Level 1

Staff Development Guide

SRA

Bothell, WA • Chicago, IL • Columbus, OH • New York, NY

MHEonline.com

 SRA

Send all inquiries to:
McGraw-Hill Education
4400 Easton Commons
Columbus, OH 43219

ISBN: 978-0-02-114667-3
MHID: 0-02-114667-5

Printed in the United States of America.

10 QVS 19

Table of Contents

Overview

Purpose

The purpose of **SRA Early Interventions in Reading** is to provide intensive small-group instruction in order to develop phonemic awareness, phonetic decoding, reading fluency, and comprehension.

SRA Early Interventions in Reading is a comprehensive reading intervention for struggling beginning readers that scaffolds elements of tasks initially beyond the student's ability, permitting the student to concentrate on and complete only those elements within their range of competence. Lessons are designed to scaffold new information in ways that allow students to assimilate and integrate the information into existing schema.

A typical lesson includes activities designed to do the following: promote phonemic awareness, provide practice sounding out decodable words composed of previously taught letter-sound correspondences, teach spelling strategies, help students develop automatic recognition of words that do not conform to alphabetic rules, and give students the opportunity to read and reread connected text composed of decodable and tricky words while applying simple, effective comprehension strategies.

In the beginning, lessons focus primarily on how to use the alphabetic principle quickly and efficiently as well as on reading connected text and reading for meaning. Later lessons emphasize decoding multisyllabic and irregular words, building reading fluency, and developing comprehension skills. As students master alphabetic elements and decoding of irregular words, the text becomes increasingly difficult but remains decodable. Comprehension strategies include explicit instruction in sequencing, making and verifying predictions, recognizing story grammar, activating prior knowledge, and identifying the main idea.

Use of Instructional Time

SRA Early Interventions in Reading maximizes academic engagement by moving lessons along in a rapid manner with constant interchange between teacher and students. "Teacher talk" is kept to a minimum, and the phrases in teaching routines are used repeatedly. Students answer questions in unison, ensuring that each student practices all content rather than watching and listening as a peer responds to you. In a typical routine, you ask all students to respond to letters, words, or text in unison and then give individual turns that allow each student to demonstrate ownership of the content. Move quickly from activity to activity within each lesson. A typical lesson includes seven to nine short activities that encompass multiple strands of content, such as phonemic awareness, alphabetic decoding and encoding, text fluency, and comprehension strategies. The time dedicated to each activity varies according to the nature of the content; yet, reading activities requiring the most time are completed in less than ten minutes. A student with a short attention span is better able to stay focused on the task at hand when activities change frequently.

Presentation Techniques

SRA Early Interventions in Reading helps achieve superior outcomes with students through the various presentation techniques for delivering instruction. For example, the small-group design for instruction, with the students sitting in a semicircle around you, allows you to more readily give directions, offer think time, and elicit student responses. Another presentation technique is maintaining a fast pace throughout the lesson and transitioning seamlessly from activity to activity within each lesson, moving as quickly as students within the group are able to progress. The objective is to keep students focused and engaged while providing daily opportunities for them to develop greater fluency in all aspects of reading and learning, including lexical retrieval, word reading, text reading, and word writing.

Clear and consistent visual and auditory cues are established to elicit responses from students. Ask for group and individual responses throughout the lesson, consistently monitoring student responses and providing praise for correct responses and immediate corrective feedback for errors. It is important to try to maintain a ratio of four praise points for every one correction. You must make on-the-spot judgments about why errors occur and must focus on that aspect of the task when providing corrective feedback. The goal is to create a classroom based on positive feedback and support for students.

To enhance students' enthusiasm for learning, provide immediate and positive feedback for each activity as students demonstrate mastery. The Mastery Sheet lists each activity within each lesson. Place a check mark on the Mastery Sheet at the end of each activity while praising students. When all the activities in a lesson are mastered, place a sticker on the Mastery Sheet for that lesson.

SRA Early Interventions in Reading defines mastery as 100 percent performance accuracy by every student, every day, on every activity. An important task is to determine when mastery has been achieved. Because the curriculum is designed to gradually and cumulatively become more complex, the majority of each lesson is composed of review and generalization work; each lesson has a mixture of review and new material. Thus, if mastery has been achieved on previous lessons, students should easily achieve mastery on new lessons. The expectation is that students begin each new activity ready to achieve at least 80 percent accuracy on their first try, with 100 percent accuracy after error corrections and scaffolding have occurred. Students demonstrate mastery during individual turns. If an error occurs during individual practice, you will provide additional instruction and additional group practice, followed by another round of individual practice. Repeat this process until all students can perform the task without errors. If a particular task proves to be very difficult for a group of students, move on to another activity, but return to the difficult task later in the same lesson or on the following day. If the activity includes a reading fluency goal, it might be necessary to reteach several activities leading up to the story to achieve the fluency goal.

Introduction to the Curriculum

Student Objectives

Each activity is designed to support the following objectives.

1. Students' ability to read and write letter-sound correspondences will be improved by attaining mastery in the daily letter-sound introduction and review activities. The most frequently encountered letter-sounds, such as *m, s, a,* and *t,* are introduced first, and the less frequent letter-sounds, such as *z, x,* and *qu,* are introduced later.

2. Students will participate in a variety of activities designed to improve their phonological awareness skills. These activities include listening for sounds within words, playing the Thumbs Up— Thumbs Down sound position game, and participating in stretching and blending activities.

3. Students will participate in activities that provide a strategy for decoding words. When they have mastered enough letter-sounds, students will sound out and read words in list form. These words are composed of the letter-sounds students have mastered thus far.

4. Students' ability to identify irregular words (referred to as "tricky words") will be improved by continuous practice and review. Students will analyze these words for sounds that follow normal patterns and those that do not.

5. When enough letter-sound correspondences and tricky words have been mastered, students will begin to read decodable text using the strategies they have learned for sounding out words. You will provide guided practice and immediate feedback during each reading. To improve and increase reading accuracy and fluency, students will reread passages as an integral part of the reading process.

6. Students will learn a variety of reading comprehension strategies, such as how to make and verify a prediction, how to use sequencing strategies, how to recognize basic story grammar, how to activate prior knowledge, and how to identify main events. You will lead these activities by asking the appropriate questions and eliciting relevant responses from the students as directed in the lessons.

7. To ensure that students are building toward the reading rate goal of an average first grader, fluency practice is built into the daily reading activity. Starting with an expected rate of 20 words per minute (wpm), students work toward a goal of 60 wpm by the end of **Teacher's Edition C.**

Student Benefits

Struggling readers must have help in order to gain proficiency in areas critical for building reading success. The ***SRA Early Interventions in Reading*** curriculum for struggling first-grade readers provides carefully designed and integrated instruction and incorporates practice in critical reading skills to help students reach mastery level. Instruction includes phonemic awareness, letter-sound correspondences, word recognition and spelling, fluency, and comprehension strategies.

Throughout the activities in all strands, specific opportunities for Language and Literacy Support are included. They provide many opportunities for students to use oral language when engaging in discussions, responding to texts, and exploring vocabulary. These would benefit students who are English language learners or students with language development deficits, including students with intellectual or developmental disabilities.

All reading activities are designed to promote success for even the lowest-performing readers. *SRA Early Interventions in Reading* is highly motivational for struggling readers. Instruction and error-correction techniques are designed to enable and motivate all students to become better readers. Systematic review of previously learned material is provided in every lesson in order to promote mastery in content areas, and maximum reading time is built in to develop reading fluency.

Without effective and early intervention, struggling readers will fall farther and farther behind their peers. The *SRA Early Interventions in Reading* curriculum provides the critical content and clear instruction needed to transform a struggling reader into a skilled reader. Results from multiple research studies confirm that after participating in this program for one year, more than 99 percent of students read at or above grade level.

Motivation

SRA Early Interventions in Reading is designed to ensure few student errors and to provide every student with the best opportunity to succeed. Lessons are structured so that students go through a constant cycle of instruction, application, and review. As the teacher, you model each skill before requiring students to perform that skill. The activities are usually performed first in unison and then individually, until each student demonstrates ownership of the skill. In this way, students make few errors and feel competent.

Working toward mastery builds a sense of confidence and success in students. Getting the answer right is very reinforcing because students feel very smart! Consistently achieving mastery develops intrinsic motivation, instilling the desire within students to learn and achieve. Students are motivated to learn new

material because they know they will soon be given the opportunity to apply what they have learned to another activity, thus demonstrating their mastery. The opportunity to successfully apply newly learned material is rewarding to students.

With *SRA Early Interventions in Reading,* praise and tangible rewards provide additional sources of motivation for students. Praise should be genuine and frequent and should be given immediately after the response being recognized. Praise should be specific and relevant to the task at hand, offering useful information to the student: for example, "I like the way you sounded out that word one sound at a time." Students then know what they did correctly and how they did it correctly so they can apply that information to the next task to achieve success again.

Tangible rewards include the use of check marks and stickers on the lesson Mastery Sheet. It is important to give check marks and stickers only when students have achieved mastery. Students are very much aware of this system and will work hard to earn the rewards.

Your level of enthusiasm when presenting the materials is another primary source of motivation. This enthusiasm engages students from the very beginning and infuses them with a feeling of anticipation and excitement about what they will learn. You are encouraged to enjoy students' successes with them and let them know that you believe in them.

Each week students receive a Time to Shine Certificate to take home that relates information to families about what students have learned that week. This also allows the parents to get involved and show their excitement for, and interest in, their child's accomplishments, which provides additional motivation to succeed.

Skilled Readers versus Struggling Readers

Skilled readers quickly read words letter by letter. Their phonological processing of words is rapid and automatic. They are able to apply decoding skills, such as looking for known parts within unknown words. Skilled readers use context clues to confirm that a word is pronounced correctly and makes sense. Skilled readers do not use context to decode unknown words.

Turning struggling readers into skilled readers requires daily, explicit, and systematic instruction that focuses on critical content. In particular, these students need to become efficient at using alphabetic information to decode unknown words and to build automatic word recognition, which in turn will facilitate fluency and comprehension. Instruction becomes cumulatively more difficult as the year progresses. Advanced skills are broken down into more manageable steps to enable student learning. Students need to achieve and experience success every day. This sense of achievement directly impacts their willingness to learn new material and to take chances in applying mastered skills in new situations. For this reason, progress is carefully monitored. Students receive constant and immediate feedback, through which they are provided with information that lets them know what they are doing correctly and how they are doing it, so they can continue applying mastered skills. Since each skill builds upon the previous one, all lessons are taught to mastery to ensure that students are able to handle each new skill before learning another.

Proof of Success

SRA Early Interventions in Reading was designed and developed by reading experts conducting research on the prevention of reading failure. The program has proven to be effective as an intervention for at-risk readers in several large-scale studies. The curriculum has since been used as the primary intervention in additional studies, including studies involving second-language learners. In each of these studies, students who participated in **SRA Early Interventions in Reading** made reading gains much greater than expected. The lowest-performing first graders in these studies scored an average of approximately 110 on multiple measures in reading on end-of-year achievement testing. This is above the national average of 100. In each study, only students initially scoring below the twentieth percentile were included. In all of the studies combined, 99.8 percent of students learned to read within the normal range for first-grade students!

Intervention Basics

The instruction is designed for small groups of three to five students. A trained intervention teacher meets with students for sessions of forty minutes a day, five days a week. The instruction is explicit and systematic in presentation. A typical lesson can be taught completely in a forty-minute session. Depending on how quickly students master the activities, you can increase the pace of the lesson or, in some cases, slow the pace. At your discretion, students are paced through a lesson at the fastest rate at which they can achieve and maintain mastery. Since the lessons are cumulative and build on each other, it is essential that each lesson be mastered before moving on to the next lesson.

Because students are receiving reading instruction in both the classroom and in the intervention, they receive a double dose of reading. This approach creates an optimal situation for students to reach their grade level in reading and to have a real chance of catching up to their peers.

Materials

CURRICULUM MATERIALS
(Program-Provided)

- Teacher's Editions A, B, C
- Activity Books A, B, C
- Answer Key
- Story-Time Readers
- Story-Time Readers Blackline Masters
- Challenge Stories
- Pictures for Language and Literacy Support

- Letter-Sound Cards
- Tricky Word Cards
- Placement and Assessment Guide (includes Lesson Mastery Sheets, Group Summary Record, and Mini Vowel and Consonant Digraph Cards)
- Maxwell (puppet)
- Staff Development Guide
- Teaching Tutor (available online only)

OTHER MATERIALS
(Teacher-Supplied)

- Timer
- Stopwatch
- Marker Board, Marker, and Eraser

- Easel
- Stickers
- Pencils

Curriculum materials include three **Teacher's Editions** and **Activity Books** for a total of 120 lessons. The list of curriculum materials helps to illustrate the different activities that contribute to making *SRA Early Interventions in Reading* a comprehensive curriculum.

You will also need the second list of materials in addition to those provided by the *SRA Early Interventions in Reading* curriculum. These materials guide you in providing the instruction at-risk students need in order to grow in ability, to stay on task, and to become skilled readers.

SRA Early Interventions in Reading: An Integrated Curriculum

The *SRA Early Interventions in Reading* curriculum is designed so that multiple strands are incorporated into all activities. Although strands are presented here separately for clarity, each strand is interwoven with the others to create a cumulative effect. The parallel strands contain skills that are embedded in more advanced skills, until each student has mastered the strand. Over the course of the intervention as the strands are mastered, they collapse into each other until students are finally on grade level and maintaining successful reading growth.

Curriculum Strands

School Year

Phonemic Awareness

Letter-Sound Correspondences

Word Recognition and Spelling

Fluency

Comprehension Strategies

Characteristics of Daily Lessons

Instruction is sequenced, and all elements are integrated. Each lesson consists of multiple strands and the skills used to teach those strands. The amount of new information introduced in any one lesson is kept to a minimum to help students as they assimilate only the immediate information. Most of each lesson is review and practice.

Classroom Arrangement

Each student needs to be able to clearly see the **Teacher's Edition** and your cues during instruction. Students need to be close enough to you to hear all instructions. Students will also need an adequate amount of space at the table to complete writing tasks in the **Activity Books.**

You should sit so that you can see all students clearly and hear all students' responses clearly. All students need to be monitored constantly and should be in easy arm's reach so you can assist with their writing activities.

Throughout the lessons there are activities in which you will need to turn quickly to the side and write on the marker board. When you model the writing of a letter for letter-sound introduction or correct an error during letter-writing and letter-sound dictation activities, you will use the marker board. In the Word Recognition and Spelling strand you will write on the board words with added endings for your students to read. In some comprehension activities you will be instructed to write student responses on either a large pad of paper or a board. Whatever you use needs to be within easy reaching distance from your seat. You do not want to have to move away from your chair or turn your back to the students when you are writing on the board. A medium-size marker board on an easel sitting to your side works very well for this.

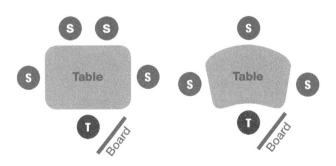

Students sit in a semicircle facing the teacher.

Strand Contents

As an integrated curriculum, the program provides an efficient framework for teaching students to read. Rather than being taught in isolation one skill at a time, multiple strands are taught in unison on a daily basis, and each strand is interrelated with the next. This design adds an element of relevancy that increases the effectiveness of the instruction.

PHONEMIC AWARENESS

- Sound Discrimination
- Oral Blending
- Stretching
- Stretch and Blend

LETTER-SOUND CORRESPONDENCES

New and Review
- Introduction
- Writing
- Review
- Dictation

FLUENCY

- Connected Text
- Story-Time Readers
- Fluency Goals
- Challenge Stories
- Partner Reading

WORD RECOGNITION AND SPELLING

- Sounding Out
- Reading Fast
- Tricky Words
- Stretch and Spell
- Chunking/Multisyllabic Words

COMPREHENSION STRATEGIES

- Retell
- Sequencing
- Story Grammar
- What I Know/Learned
- Main Idea

Staff Development Guide, Level 1

Scope and Sequence

A scope and sequence chart can be found in the front matter of each **Teacher's Edition.** This chart allows you to see at a glance which instructional strands are being taught in a given lesson and the skills being taught for the strands.

To read the scope and sequence chart, locate the first lesson in the chart. Read across the row following the numeral 1 to see which specific skills are being taught in the first lesson of the intervention. To identify the strand each skill belongs with, look for the strand name at the top of the column. For example, initial sound blending is a skill used to teach Phonemic Awareness in the first lesson. In the Letter-Sound Correspondences strand, the letter-sound *Mm* is introduced. In the Fluency strand, the group reads a story.

Level 1

SCOPE AND SEQUENCE

Lesson Introduced	Phonemic Awareness	Letter-Sound Correspondences	Word Recognition and Spelling		Fluency	Comprehension Strategies
			Word Types	Tricky Words		
1	• Initial Sound	• Mm			• Story Reading	
2	• VC Pattern • CVC Pattern • Last Sound			• I	• Choral Story Reading	
3	• CVC Pattern (continuous) • Middle Sound	• Aa (short)				
4				• the • The • VC Words		
5	• CVC Pattern (stop)	• Tt				
6			• CVC Words (continuous)		• Connected Text	
7		• Ss			• Connected Text	
8			• Plurals—s	• is • Is	• Connected Text	
9	• CVCC Pattern (continuous)	• Rr			• Connected Text	
10				• on	• Connected Text • Story-Time Reader 1, *The Baby,* Chapter 1	• Story Prediction
11		• Dd			• Connected Text	
12	• CVCC Pattern (stop)			• A • a • are	• Connected Text	• Oral Story Retell

Appendix 1 Scope and Sequence

Fully Specified Lessons

The lesson dialogues in the **Teacher's Editions** act as a guide for the teacher. They are prescriptive and highly detailed, and they spell out every aspect of each activity. Each lesson is designed to communicate only what the students need to learn that particular day. Teaching formats are presented in clear and consistent language, and they have been thoroughly tested in various studies to ensure success.

Routines

Using consistent formats reduces student confusion and enhances student learning. The formats are specific to the different strands. As students master skills, the formats evolve over time to accommodate students' continual progression toward becoming successful and fluent readers. By planning each lesson ahead of time, you ensure that instruction is consistently clear and guesswork on the part of students is reduced. The overarching teaching routine repeated throughout the curriculum is composed of the following steps: modeling new content, providing guided practice, and implementing individual practice in every activity. Preview and prepare for each lesson before its presentation to be clear about what is expected of both you and students in each activity.

Format Presentation

The lesson dialogues include what you say, what the correct student response is, and how you should respond based on the accuracy of the students' responses.

Present lessons in a natural way, without necessarily reading the dialogue word by word. You may slightly alter the wording as long as you preserve the intended specific instructional goal of each activity. Try to maintain eye contact as much as possible with your students throughout the lesson presentation.

A sample activity is displayed on the next page. As you review the sample activity, you will see that the **Teacher's Editions** use three different typefaces so you can easily recognize each part of the activity at a glance:

Bold blue type indicates what you say.

Bold red type indicates what the students say.

(Italic blue type in parentheses indicates what you do.)

Look at the sample activity on the next page.

Look for dialogue that is written in bold blue type: **What is this letter's sound?** This is what you say to your students.

Look for dialogue that is written in bold red type: **/nnn/.** This is the correct answer that you want to hear from your students. If you don't get the correct answer, then you will need to provide an error correction. Specific error corrections are discussed later in this guide.

Look for dialogue that is written blue and in italics: *(When you go through the list of words, distinguish between the letters* m *and* n *before sounding out each word.)* This is what you do. Any necessary cues appear in blue and italic also. You may be asked to model a skill for the students. These directions will vary from activity to activity, but they will be written in italic type also so that you will know at a glance what you are supposed to do.

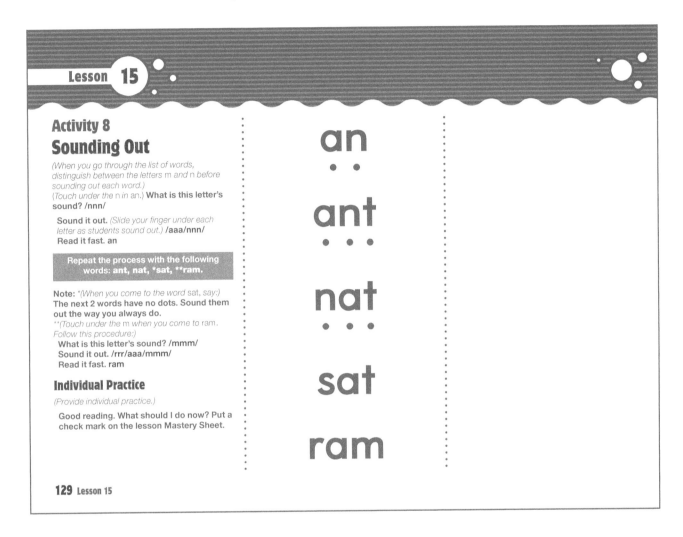

Lesson 15

Activity 8
Sounding Out

(When you go through the list of words, distinguish between the letters m *and* n *before sounding out each word.)*
(Touch under the n *in an.)* **What is this letter's sound? /nnn/**

Sound it out. *(Slide your finger under each letter as students sound out.)* **/aaa/nnn/**
Read it fast. an

> Repeat the process with the following words: ant, nat, *sat, **ram.

Note: **(When you come to the word* sat, *say:)* **The next 2 words have no dots. Sound them out the way you always do.**
**(Touch under the m *when you come to* ram. *Follow this procedure:)*
What is this letter's sound? /mmm/
Sound it out. /rrr/aaa/mmm/
Read it fast. ram

Individual Practice

(Provide individual practice.)

Good reading. What should I do now? Put a check mark on the lesson Mastery Sheet.

an

ant

nat

sat

ram

129 Lesson 15

Activity Tracking Chart

An activity tracking chart is located in the appendix of each **Teacher's Edition.** This chart allows you to see where each specific skill, letter-sound correspondence, tricky word, or story is introduced and taught within the curriculum. For instance, as shown in the chart below, in Lessons 1–10 the letter-sound correspondences *Mm, Aa, Tt, Ss,* and *Rr* are introduced and reviewed.

ACTIVITY TRACK: Teacher's Edition A, Lessons 1–40

Lesson	Rhyme Time	Adding Endings	Letter-Sound (New/Review)	Sound Discrimination/Position	Stretching	Oral Blending	Stretch & Blend	Sounding Out	Write Sound/Spell Words	Tricky Words	Fluency	Comprehension
1	★		• Mm	• Beginning Sound	★				★		• Story Reading	
2	★		• Review	• Beginning and Ending Sounds	★	★		★	★	• I • Review	• Choral Story Reading	
3			• Aa • Review	• Beginning and Ending Sounds	★	★	★		★	• Review		
4			• Review	• Beginning Sound	★	★	★	★	★	• the • The • Review		
5			• Tt • Review	• Beginning and Ending Sounds	★	★	★	★	★	• Review		
6			• Review	• Beginning and Ending Sounds			★	★	★	• Review	• Connected Text	
7			• Ss • Review	• Beginning and Ending Sounds			★	★	★	• Review	• Connected Text	
8			• Review	• Beginning and Ending Sounds			★	★	★	• is • Is • Review	• Connected Text	
9			• Rr • Review	• Beginning Sound			★	★	★	• Review	• Connected Text	
10			• Review				★	★	★	• on • Review	• Connected Text • Story-Time Reader 1, *The Baby,* Chapter 1	• Story Prediction

Appendix 9 Activity Track Chart

Critical Features

There are three critical features for successful implementation of the materials: pacing, error correction, and teaching to mastery. All three must be present to achieve the level of success possible with the program.

A well-paced lesson promotes the development of fluency and retention. Students are provided every minute of instruction with many opportunities to respond, ensuring that each student gets enough practice with concepts and skills to gain ownership of the practiced content.

Pacing

Instructional Pacing

Instructional pacing is a critical factor in the presentation of these lessons and can make or break the effectiveness of instruction. The objective is to go as fast as the students can go, without going faster than they can handle. In a well-paced lesson the dialogue between you and the students occurs as a rapid interchange. Fast pacing greatly increases academic engagement because students pay closer attention to the material being presented, which, in turn, increases learning by reducing behavior problems and keeping students involved and on task.

Good Pacing

Pacing should be fast enough to keep students attending and on task, but not so fast that they begin to guess and make errors. Pacing should be rapid. When students respond correctly, move quickly to the next instance or task. There should be minimal extraneous language—from you or the students—or off-task behavior during transitions. With good pacing, you will be able to elicit about eight to ten responses per minute from each student! If the pacing is appropriate, students receive more practice time and have an increased opportunity for achieving success.

Ensuring Academic Responses with Cues

To achieve good pacing, you use a variety of cues. A cue indicates when students answer. Cues used to elicit student responses are either visual or auditory.

- Visual cues are used when the students are looking at you or at the **Teacher's Edition.**
- Auditory cues are used when the students are working from their **Activity Books** or reading from their **Story-Time Readers.**

Using cues helps you control pacing and provide appropriate think time for students before they answer. The use of cues minimizes students' tendency to guess or blurt out incorrect answers when they do not take time to think before answering.

The basic routine of each activity includes unison responses followed by individual practice. Students feel safer when answering in unison. Unison responses provide maximum opportunity for students to practice each skill as it is being taught. Cueing is an effective technique for keeping students together and for increasing automaticity of response.

Different formats require different cues. Be consistent to help students learn which cue is associated with each of the skills. Clarity of cues is essential to ensure that you move smoothly through tasks during instructional time. You will quickly find the cues that work best with your teaching style. The key is to be consistent with the cues and to keep them crisp and quick.

TYPES OF CUES

STRAND	RECOMMENDED CUE
All strands	**Hand Drop:** Cue is used to ensure that students will think before they provide an answer to a question. It can be used to elicit individual or unison responses. **Implementation of cue:** As you ask a question, hold your hand at shoulder level with your palm facing outward. Give approximately two seconds of think time, and then drop your hand with a slashing motion indicating that you are ready for the students' answer.
Phonemic Awareness	**First Sound:** Cue enables students to identify the first sound they hear within a word. **Implementation of cue:** Hold your right fist at shoulder level so the back of your hand is facing the students. Raise your index finger, cueing students to say the sound while reinforcing left-to-right directionality.
Phonemic Awareness	**Stretching Words:** Cue enables students to identify each sound they hear within a word. **Implementation of cue:** Hold your right fist at shoulder level so the back of your hand is facing the students, and hold up one finger for each sound within a word.
Letter-Sound Correspondences	**Point-Touch:** Cue guides students as they say each sound in a letter-sound review activity. **Implementation of cue:** Point to the letter-sound, pause, and touch under the letter-sound for students to read. Students say the sound as you touch under each letter-sound. Students hold the sound for as long as you touch under the letter or letter combination. Hold your finger under the letter-sound for two to three seconds for continuous sounds; touch quickly under stop sounds.
Word Recognition and Spelling	**Sounding Out/Read It:** Cue guides students as they read words. **Implementation of cue:** When having students sound out words, use the point-touch cue as described above, moving from left to right underneath the word. Guide students as they read the word by quickly sliding your finger under the word, moving from left to right.
Fluency	**Text Pacing:** This cue is used when students read aloud in unison. It controls the pace of the reading and keeps students together. **Implementation of cue:** Softly tap your finger or the eraser end of a pencil on the table for each word you want students to read. The rhythm should resemble that of a metronome, softly tapping at intervals of every two to three seconds or at a pace listed in the dialogue for the reading activity.

You will establish four rules from the very beginning to prepare students to observe and to respond properly to cueing: Sit tall; Listen big; Answer when I cue; and Answer together. A quick reminder is inserted in lesson presentation dialogues whenever necessary.

Error Corrections

It is important to give immediate corrective feedback to your students when they make an error. This means all errors are corrected as soon as they occur.

Error Correction: Basic Facts

A "basic fact" is anything that has no steps to achieving an answer and has only one right answer. Basic facts include naming letter-sound correspondences, identifying the first sound of a word, and automatically reading irregular sight words.

When an error occurs on a basic fact, model the fact by telling the fact: **My turn. The sound for this letter is /sss/.** When you model, you literally do the task for the students, showing them how the task is done. Next, you ask *all* the students to repeat the item: **Your turn.** Last, you back up a few items and restart the activity: **Let's back up and do that again.** By backing up one to two items, you are letting a little time pass between the correcting technique and retesting the group and/or the student on it. Error corrections are taught to the entire group, regardless of which student committed the error. This prevents confusion and allows all students to practice the correct response again. The lesson continues to move smoothly, and all students remain engaged.

Error Correction: Complex Tasks

When tasks have multiple steps, a "lead step" is added to the correction procedure. Examples of complex tasks include stretching and blending, segmenting a word into separate phonemes and then blending it back together, and sounding out a word and then reading it fast.

When an error is made on a complex task, first model the correct answer: **My turn.** Then lead the students: **Do it with me.** Then test students on the same item again: **Your turn.** Finally, back up one to two items and restart the activity: **Let's back up and begin again.**

ERROR CORRECTION TECHNIQUES

Model: "My turn"	Model: "My turn"
Lead: "Do it with me"	Test: "Your turn"
Test: "Your turn"	Retest: "Let's back up"
Retest: "Let's back up"	

Scaffolding

As students advance, you will not always want to model an entire series of steps when an error occurs on a complex task. Instead, you will provide scaffolding, leading students to use what they know to determine the correct answer without totally depending on you. Scaffolding requires on-the-spot teacher judgment. When you scaffold, you determine what piece of knowledge is needed to move the student to the correct answer.

For example, suppose that during letter-sound dictation activities, a student spells incorrectly the word *rock* with a *c* at the end, *roc*. You would remind the student that there is more than one way to spell the /k/ sound, and that the correct spelling is typically used at the end of a word. If at this point the student cannot remember the variant spelling, then revert to a more direct error correction technique. Show the student the letter-sound card for that sound, point to the correct spelling for that letter-sound correspondence, and have the student make the necessary correction. There is not one right way, so scaffolding depends on good judgment from the teacher. When in doubt, use the Model-Lead-Test correction technique.

Mastery

Every activity in every lesson is taught to mastery. Teaching to mastery ensures that students will be ready to move forward in the strand without the lessons becoming too difficult. Mastery communicates that what is learned today is important because it will be needed in later lessons.

A skill is considered mastered when every student is able to perform the skill independently without making any mistakes. The goal in each activity is to teach the skills to mastery before moving to the next activity. However, there may be a time when the students are having difficulty with a certain activity. In this instance, you may say, **This is really hard; let's go on and come back to this later.** This should not occur often, but it is acceptable on rare occasions as long as you return to that activity before completing the lesson.

Determining Mastery

Mastery is assessed and determined mostly during the independent practice portion of the activities. Each student in the group must demonstrate the skill during independent practice with no errors. If a student makes an error, use the appropriate correction procedure, and practice the specific skill repeatedly until the student has mastered it. If a student needs any assistance, mastery has not been achieved.

Individual Practice

Provide every student an individual turn at the end of each activity. It is during individual practice that you determine whether each student has truly mastered the activity or if you need to provide additional group practice. As a rule, if more than two errors occur during individual practice, the group needs more practice.

Conducting Individual Practice

After group responses, call on each student individually to complete a few items or read a few sentences. Give each student one to three items during individual practice. You may need to give a stronger student only one item, but a weaker student two or three items to ensure mastery. Typically you should call on lower-performing students first. Then you will call on a higher-performing student while encouraging the other students to answer in their heads. When all students can complete the task independently and without error, you know the group has achieved 100 percent mastery.

Lesson Mastery Sheet

At the end of each activity, tell students whether they have mastered the skill being taught. If they have, you will put a check mark on the lesson Mastery Sheet. This check indicates that every student in the group demonstrated mastery for the skill independently with no mistakes. If an error occurs during individual practice, provide additional instruction and additional group practice followed by another round of individual turns. Repeat this process until all students are able to perform the skill independently without error. At the end of each lesson, when all skills in the lesson have been mastered, place a sticker in the Mastery column to indicate mastery of the entire lesson.

Lesson Mastery Sheet

Teacher_____ Group_____

Students_____   _____

_____   _____

_____   _____

Activity	1	2	3	4	5	6	7	8	9	10	Fluency		Mastery
1									★	★			
2													
3									★	★			
4													
5													
6								★	★	★			
7										★			
8									★	★			
9													
10										★			

(Left row label: Lesson)

Placement and Assessment Guide, Level 1

8   Mastery Sheet

Make one copy for each group of students.

When Mastery Is Hard to Achieve

Occasionally it will be hard for the group to achieve mastery on a specific activity. If you sense that students are becoming frustrated, note the activity on the Mastery Sheet, and move to the next activity. You may need to leave the activity temporarily, but return to complete the activity later in the lesson or at the beginning of the next lesson.

Do *not* place a sticker on the Mastery Sheet for the lesson until mastery has been achieved. If students are still unable to achieve mastery, you may need to back up a lesson or two to review the activities that led up to the specific skill causing difficulty. If one student is having difficulty mastering a skill, it is best to find a few extra minutes to work with that student individually.

Measuring Mastery Through Progress Monitoring

A series of student assessments is provided to assess mastery of the skills presented in each of the **Teacher's Editions.** Students are assessed for mastery and generalization of letter-sound correspondences, word reading, and connected text. An assessment is administered every sixth or eighth lesson. Each of the first six assessments is timed for one minute. Starting in **Teacher's Edition B,** students also read a passage they have previously read. The teacher times the student for one minute. Fluency is calculated as words correct per minute (wcpm), with the fluency goal for the assessments listed in the teacher's materials.

These in-program assessments are a powerful tool for monitoring students' progress and evaluating your presentation of lesson content. The assessments help you determine whether students are learning what you are teaching, whether your lesson-presentation pacing is appropriate, and when to reteach. As mentioned in the section on the Lesson Mastery Sheet, the student assessments are also valuable tools for ensuring that students

who were previously making progress on skills have mastered those skills before moving on to the next set of lessons. This will ensure that students can build on the mastered skills from previous lessons with the new skills taught in the new lessons.

Placing Students in SRA Early Interventions in Reading

To appropriately place students in the **SRA Early Interventions in Reading** program, administer a reliable and valid screening measure during the first several weeks of the school year. Many schools and classrooms are beginning to give such tests routinely to all children at the beginning of the year. If such tests are not routine in your school, initial teacher observations can be helpful in spotting children who should be screened to determine if they would benefit from **SRA Early Interventions in Reading.**

One quick way to spot students likely to need this intervention is to watch for students who are struggling to master the letter-sound, blending, and decoding instruction provided during the first several weeks of the school year. Students who consistently struggle with phonemic awareness activities during instruction may also need the extra help provided by the program. Of course, it becomes easier to notice students who are not making adequate progress as each week passes. However, it is important to identify students who need extra help as soon as possible because every day that passes allows students to fall farther and farther behind their peers. Our goal for all students is grade-level reading skills by the end of the year; the farther behind children fall at any point in the year, the more difficult it is for them to achieve that goal.

Several currently available tests can be used to screen students who need the support provided in **SRA Early Interventions in Reading.** These tests are described in more detail in the **Teacher's Editions.**

Placing students in the appropriate lessons is essential to ensuring student success in *SRA Early Interventions in Reading.* When a student has been identified as potentially benefiting from an early intervention curriculum, through either an outside test of skills or by teacher observations, administer the Placement Test. The Placement Test consists of a series of short activities that mirror the content of the intervention materials at different points in the curriculum. Based on a student's demonstrated mastery of the skills in each Placement Test section, you administer the next section, place the student in a specific lesson in the curriculum, or move him or her out of the intervention group to receive instruction in only the primary reading materials.

Time to Shine

Each week, send home with students a Time to Shine Reading Certificate. On it you will list the new letter-sound correspondences, word types, and stories the student has read and mastered that week. Attach a copy of the take-home version of the **Story-Time Readers** students read during the week. Students are required to read these stories to an adult in the home. The Time to Shine Reading Certificate and take-home **Story-Time Readers** establish a connection between the teacher and the student's parents or guardian. A blackline master version of the Time to Shine Reading Certificate, in both English and Spanish, is in the **Placement and Assessment Guide.**

Reflective Teaching

Even though *SRA Early Interventions in Reading* is very structured, you will still need to reflect on your teaching to understand why your instruction is or is not having the desired effect with specific students. The purpose of this reflection is to gain awareness of your teaching practices and to formulate a plan of action to improve instruction as needed. It may help to keep a journal to document

successes and challenges. (Journal entries should be made immediately after a lesson is finished and not during the actual lesson.) Over time, in these entries you will see recurring patterns as you reflect on your students' needs. It is also helpful to discuss successes and challenges with colleagues, intervention coaches, or other educators.

As you make decisions about how to adapt your instruction to meet the needs of your students, be careful to maintain the instruction's integrity and preserve each activity's intended goal. Always consider the lesson's or activity's objectives to determine whether your students are progressing toward accomplishing the objectives.

Teaching Special Populations

Reflective teaching and adapting the lessons are particularly important when teaching special populations of students, such as students at risk for developing learning disabilities, students with intellectual disabilities, and English language learners. Although lesson structure and pacing are designed to benefit such learners, use the curriculum flexibly to meet your students' needs.

Language and Literacy Support

Specific opportunities for language and literacy support are in every lesson. They are designed specifically for English Language Learners; however, they will benefit all students who struggle with oral language. Language and Literacy support appears most frequently in word recognition, fluency, and comprehension activities. You will present new vocabulary words; students will discuss the words, giving you the opportunity to clarify any misunderstandings. You will use pictures from the selections as well as additional photographs in **Pictures for Language and Literacy Support** to support vocabulary development.

The Phonology of English

While English has twenty-six letters in its alphabet, it is composed of many more than twenty-six speech sounds. Linguists estimate that English has between forty-two and forty-four different sounds, and this number may be slightly higher or lower depending on many variables, including regional and individual differences in speech and changes in how sounds are stressed. These individual speech sounds are called phonemes. A phoneme is the smallest unit of sound that can make a difference in meaning. The conventions for spelling the forty-four phonemes in English pose a very difficult task for many children and even for some adults. English sounds have hundreds of graphemes, or written representations of sounds. Take, for example, the five vowels, *a, e, i, o, u.* These five letters are but the tip of the iceberg. There are actually eighteen vowel phonemes in English, and there are eighty ways they are commonly spelled (eighty common graphemes). Think about how these eighteen vowel phonemes sound. For example, consider all the differences in your lip and tongue positions when you say these words: *three, cake, ought, moon, hat, coil.* Notice that your lips are pursed, stretched, or open. Your tongue is either touching your teeth, between your teeth, just behind your teeth, or on the roof of your mouth. Consider the many different graphemes that helped spell those vowel sounds: $\overline{\overline{ee}}$, *a_e, ough,* $\overline{oo}$, *a, oi.*

Consonant phonemes comprise the other twenty-six sounds of English. In some ways, the spelling of consonant phonemes is less complicated than the spelling of vowel phonemes in English, because there is a one-to-one correspondence between the letter and sound for eighteen of the consonant phonemes. In other words, the /d/ sound is spelled with a *d.* The /t/ sound is spelled with a *t,* and so on. There are seven consonant phonemes that are represented by two letters. (For example, the /sh/ sound is spelled *sh;* the /ch/ sound is spelled *ch.*) These are called digraphs because the two-letter spelling represents a phoneme. They are sometimes confused with consonant blends, which are simply two or more consonant phonemes side by side, with each retaining its original sound. (The blend of /str/ is made up of three phonemes: /s/, /t/, and /r/.) Some consonants do not have a unique phoneme assigned to them, including *c, q,* and *x.* The letter *c* represents either the /k/ sound or /s/ sound, the letter *q* represents the /kw/ sound, and the letter *x* represents the /ks/ sound.

Finally, consonant phonemes are divided into voiced and unvoiced sounds. In voiced consonants, the vocal cords vibrate. For example, *zoo* sounds different from Sue because the *z* is voiced. In contrast, in unvoiced consonants, the vocal cords do not vibrate: *pit, fit.* Have students put their hands on their vocal cords to feel the vibration. Often, in the American dialect of English, unvoiced consonants like *t* that are sandwiched between two voiced vowels are "voiced": *biting* and *butter* can sound like *biding* and *budder.* These are called "flaps," and many speakers of British English do not use this pronunciation.

Teaching and the Phonology of English

Up to this point, the discussion of the phonology of English has relied on some technical language, such as phoneme, grapheme, digraph, and blend. However, when teaching children, we want to stress that such formal language is *not* used. Students do not need to know the theoretical concepts, but they are instead encouraged to develop automaticity in recognizing different letter-sound combinations. As you teach the **SRA Early Interventions in Reading** curriculum, you will inevitably become increasingly familiar with the structure of English because the curriculum is carefully laid out to follow certain principles of English phonology. To help you develop some of this background knowledge—or to refresh you on what you might have learned already—we will review some of the major components and terms of the phonology of English that are particularly useful when teaching the **SRA Early Interventions in Reading** curriculum.

Continuous and Stop Sounds

Continuous sounds are sounds that can be held, hummed, or sung. The most obvious continuous sounds are vowels; all vowel sounds are continuous, including long and short vowels, *r*-controlled vowels (vowels that change their sounds slightly when followed by *r*), diphthongs (a blend of vowels in one syllable, such as *oy* in *boy* and *ow* in *now*), and *schwa* (the vowel sound sometimes heard in an unstressed syllable). Continuous consonants include *f, l, m, n, q(u), r, s, v, w, x, y, z*. When you are teaching the **SRA Early Interventions in Reading** curriculum, you will hold the continuous sounds for two to three seconds. Holding continuous sounds makes sounding out and reading words fast easier for students.

Stop sounds are sounds that block the passage of air as the sound is completed. You cannot hold the /t/ sound, for example, because the very act of making the sound stops the flow of air. The stop sounds are all consonants: *b, c, d, g, h, j, k, p, t*. Say the stop sounds quickly without distorting the sound. For example, the /b/ sound should not be distorted by the sound /uh/ at the end of it.

Syllable Types

A syllable is a unit of pronunciation that has one and only one vowel sound. There are six common syllable types in English spelling: closed, open, *r*-controlled, vowel team, silent *e*, and consonant *-le*. Students are never explicitly taught the labels for each of these; however, the curriculum is written with a clear understanding of these syllable types so students are exposed to all of them.

Closed: The vowel sound is usually short, and the single vowel is usually followed by a consonant *(cat, rabbit)*.

Open: A syllable ends with a single vowel sound, which is usually long *(me, tree)*.

***r*-controlled:** The vowel in the syllable is followed by an *r*, which changes its sound so that the sound is not long or short *(heart, danger)*.

Vowel team: Two or more letters together make a single vowel sound in the syllable *(rain, head, spoil)*. Notice that these can be long, short, or diphthongs.

Silent *e*: A syllable with the vowel-consonant-silent *e* pattern: *(make, rope)*

Some terms like long *e* and short *e*, which are probably familiar to you, are avoided in this curriculum. Instead, students are taught to develop automaticity and to recognize the sounds they see, not the labels that go with the rules.

The Sound Pronunciation Guide on the following pages corresponds to the sounds and spellings taught in **SRA Early Interventions in Reading.**

Sound Pronunciation Guide

/aaa/	lamb, am	/a̅a̅a̅/	age	/b/	ball, bat, cab
		_a	label, baby		
		_ai	bait, mail, aid		
		_ay	day, play, away		
		a_e	vane, lane		
		eigh	eight, weigh		
		ea	break, great		
/k/	camera	/d/	dinosaur, dad	/eee/	hen, red
c	cat, car			ea	head, bread
k	kitten, kite				
ck	pack, sack				
/e̅e̅e̅/	eat	/fff/	fan	/g/	gopher, dog
_e	be, he	f	fish, if		
ee	seed, feed	ph	photo, phone		
ea	read, bead				
e_e	eve				
_y	very, happy				
_ie	families				
/h/	hound, hat	/iii/	pig, it	/i̅i̅i̅/	icy
				i	item, ivy
				_y	my, reply
				i_e	pine, ride
				_ie	tie, pie, flies
				_igh	right, light
/j/	jump	/lll/	lion	/mmm/	monkey
j	jar, major	l	lake, tall	m	man, yummy
ge	gentle, page	-le	bottle, apple	_mb	climb, limb
_dge	bridge, ridge				
gi	giant				
/nnn/	nose	/ooo/	frog, on	/o̅o̅o̅/	open
n	not, sun			o	over, go
kn_	knot, knee			_ow	own, grow
				o_e	note, rode
				oa_	oak, toad
				_oe	toe, doe
/p/	popcorn, map	/qu/	quack, queen	/rrr/	robot
				r	run, red
				wr_	wrap, wrong

Sound Pronunciation Guide

/sss/	sausage	/t/	timer, Tom, toast	/u/	tug, up
s	so, pass				
ce	cent, face				
ci_	circle, city				
/ūuū/	use	/vvv/	vacuum, velvet	/www/	washer, wow
u	unit, menu				
_ew	few, pew				
u_e	cube, fuse				
_ue	cue, fuel				
/ks/	exit, ax, fox	/yyy/	yaks, yes, yell	/zzz/	zipper
				z	zoo, maze
				_s	was, laws
/sh/	shark, ship, mash	/arr/	armadillo, car, jar	/th/	feather, that, them
/ch/	chipmunk	/err/	bird	/ing/	king, sing
ch	cherry, church	er	farmer, fern		
_tch	crutch, patch	ir	dirt, stir		
		ur	fur, burn		
/th/	thimble, think, three	/wh/	whales, white	/all/	ball
				al	also, almost
				all	call, tall
/or/	corn, form, order	/ol/	cold, told, old	**-ed, pronounced**	
				/ed/	handed, glided
				/d/	filled, named
				/t/	hoped, roped
/ow/	cow	/aw/	hawk	/ōo/	goo
ow	down, howl	aw	jaw, dawn	oo	too, roof
ou_	loud, out	au_	caught, sauce	_ew	blew, new
				_ue	blue, glue
				u_e	rule, tube
				o	do, who
				ui	suit, fruit
				oe	shoe, canoe
				u	tuna, ruby
/ŏŏ/	foot	/oi/	coil	ere	here
oo	soot	oi	boil, coin	eer	deer
u	put, bush	_oy	boy, toy	ear	hear
_are	care, share				

Strand One: Phonemic Awareness

In the Phonemic Awareness Strand, students listen to and manipulate sounds within words, which lays the foundation for learning letter-sound correspondences and for word-recognition skills. In this strand, students learn to segment words into individual sounds and to blend the sounds back into words before sounding out whole words. Later, students will listen for each sound they hear in a word and spell each sound in the order they hear it.

You will notice in the activities illustrated in this section that students are never asked to look at words or to map sounds to visual symbols. Instead, they develop auditory sensitivity to the sounds they will later learn to match to written letters when decoding words. This auditory sensitivity, which helps students notice and distinguish sounds in speech, will greatly benefit them in later lessons as they begin to map the sounds they hear to written alphabetic symbols.

Phonemic Awareness is carefully sequenced to facilitate learning. Students move from easier to harder skills as they progress across lessons. Initial sound recognition is taught first because this is the easiest sound for students to distinguish in a word, followed by last sounds, and then medial sounds. Students then progress through Auditory Blending, Segmenting, Stretching and Blending, and Vowel Discrimination, as one skill builds upon the next.

Phonemic Awareness (Teacher's Edition A)

Several typical activities in the Phonemic Awareness Strand in the first part of the school year come from the two categories Sound Discrimination and Segmentation and Blending, which are discussed more fully on the next pages in the order they are introduced in the curriculum.

FORMATS

- Sound Discrimination
  - First-Sound Game
  - Sound Position: Thumbs Up—Thumbs Down
- Segmentation and Blending
  - Oral Blending
  - Stretching Words
  - Stretch and Blend

All the phonemic awareness activities in **Teacher's Edition A** have one thing in common. They all include a special "modeling" phase in which you introduce students to the new activities. At the beginning stage, you are teaching students not just the concepts (in this case the concepts involved in developing phonemic awareness) but also your techniques for working with them on learning the new concepts. For example, in the first phonemic awareness activity described below, First-Sound Game, you model for your students both how to identify the first sounds of words and how to play the game itself. Over time, your students will learn how to play the game, so this modeling strategy will be phased out.

After the activity has been adequately modeled, your students will no longer need the model, so you will be using a basic activity structure. This basic activity structure appears in this guide as a series of steps labeled "Activity at a Glance."

Phonemic Awareness (Teacher's Edition A): Sound Discrimination

There are two basic sound discrimination formats: First-Sound Game and Sound Position. In these, students learn to distinguish between sounds within words and to identify sound position within words (beginning, ending, or middle). There are two variations of Sound Position: "beginning or ending" and "thumbs up—thumbs down."

First-Sound Game

Because the beginning sounds of words are the easiest for students to distinguish, students listen for those from the very first day of the intervention. This also allows students to connect initial sounds of key words later when learning letter-sound correspondences.

The format for teaching the First-Sound Game is very straightforward. Say a word, emphasizing the first sound in that word. Say the word so students hear the first sound distinctly. Ask your students, **What is the first sound?** Cue the students to answer together by quickly holding up your index finger. It is important that you do not mouth sounds with students when it is their turn to answer. Repeat the procedure with the remaining words.

ACTIVITY AT A GLANCE

- Step 1: Tell your students they are going to be listening for a sound at the beginning, at the end, or in the middle of a word. You will be working with only one sound position at a time within the word.

- Step 2: Say a word, emphasizing the sound you want your students to hear. Say it in such a way that the students can hear that sound distinctly from the rest of the word, for example, */sss/un.*

- Step 3: Ask your students to tell you what sound they hear in the specified position within a word: **What is the first sound you hear in the word */sss/un?***

- Step 4: Give your students a second or two of think time, and then cue them to respond in unison by holding up your index finger. Do not say the sound with them.

- Step 5: Repeat the procedure with the remaining words. **New word, */mmm/ arble.* What is the first sound in */mmm/arble?* Cue the students to answer. Correct all errors as they occur.

- Step 6: End with individual mastery check by giving each student one or two words.

IN THE REAL WORLD

Sometimes students give the letter's *name* instead of the *sound* for the answer. They say *em* instead of */mmm/.* Model how to say the *sound* and not the letter's *name.* Have students practice saying the sound.

Students catch on to this game rather quickly. The first sounds are usually easy for them, but the ending and middle sounds are often more difficult. If students are unable to identify a sound, correct by stretching the word. For example, sometimes they will listen for the last sound in a word: **Listen while I stretch the word mouse, */mmm/ou/sss/.*** Tap on the finger that is raised for the last sound in the word and ask again, **What's the**

last sound you hear in *mou/sss/?* Because students are having trouble identifying the correct sound, you may need to emphasize the sound by holding it a little longer than usual.

When in doubt, correct with the Model-Lead-Test strategy.

Questions and Answers

Activity 3

First-Sound Game

We are now ready to play First Sound. Remember, I say a word, and then you tell me the first sound you hear in the word. Get ready to listen big.

Here is the first word. *(Say the first sound slowly to emphasize it. Hold it 2–3 seconds.)* **/Sss/un.**

What is the first sound in **/sss/un?** *(Cue students by holding up one finger.)* **/sss/** Very good. The first sound we hear in **sun** is **/sss/.**

Next word. *(Pause.)* **/Mmm/arble.** *(Pause.)* What is the first sound in **/mmm/arble?** **/mmm/** *(Monitor and correct.)*

Right. Next word. *(Pause.)* **/Fff/an.** *(Pause.)* What is the first sound in **/fff/an?** **/fff/**

Repeat this format with the following words: beat, feel, mouse, nut.

(Scaffold as necessary.)

Individual Practice

(Provide individual practice with 1–2 words per student.)

Great job hearing the first sound. I will put a check mark on the lesson Mastery Sheet so we can go to our next activity.

35 Lesson 4

Sound Position: Thumbs Up—Thumbs Down

In this activity, students listen to words and say whether the words begin or end with a specific sound. If a word starts with the target sound, students hold their thumbs in an up position. If the word does not start with the target sound, students hold their thumbs in a down position.

ACTIVITY AT A GLANCE

- Step 1: Tell your students they are going to play a game to help them listen for a sound at the beginning of a word.
- Step 2: Remind students of the rules of the game. If they hear the sound at the beginning of the word, they will put their thumbs up. If they do not hear the sound at the beginning of the word, they will put their thumbs down.
- Step 3: As you say the word, emphasize the sound you want your students to identify, so they can hear that sound distinctly from the rest of the word: */rrr/abbit.*

- Step 4: Repeat the word, emphasizing the sound, and cue students to put their thumbs up or down according to whether they hear the sound at the beginning of the word.
- Step 5: Repeat the procedure with the remaining words. Remember to correct all errors as soon as they occur.
- Step 6: End with individual mastery check by giving each student one or two words.

IN THE REAL WORLD

Students usually love this game. Another way to play the Thumbs Up—Thumbs Down game is to have your students put their heads down, close their eyes, and place their hands flat on the table as they listen for the sound.

Correct errors with Model-Test error-correction technique.

Questions and Answers

Activity 3

Thumbs Up— Thumbs Down

Beginning Sound

(Hold up the Rr letter-sound card. Point to r.) **What sound is this?** /rrr/

Good job remembering the letter-sound /rrr/. **Now we are going to play the Thumbs Up—Thumbs Down game. I will say some words.**

If the word begins with the /rrr/ **sound, put your thumbs up. If the word does not begin with** /rrr/, **put your thumbs down.**

Everybody, show me what you will do if the word begins with the /rrr/ **sound.** *(Students should put their thumbs up.)*

Very good! You will put your thumbs up if the word begins with the /rrr/ **sound.**

Get ready to listen big. *(Optional: Heads down or eyes closed.)* **Hands flat on the table. First word.** *(Pause.)* **Radio.** *(Pause.)* **Does** *radio* **begin with the** /rrr/ **sound?** *(Students should put their thumbs up).*

> **Repeat the process with the following words: rabbit, basket, rip, race, slip, clown, rotten.**

Individual Practice

(Provide individual practice. Students may answer aloud during individual practice.)

Excellent work! I will check off this activity on the Mastery Sheet.

Phonemic Awareness (Teacher's Edition A): Segmentation and Blending

There are three formats focusing on phonemic segmentation and blending: Oral Blending, Segmenting, and Stretch and Blend. Blending is combining sounds in order to make a whole word. Segmentation is the separation of a word into its individual sounds. Practicing segmenting further promotes auditory sensitivity to individual phonemes in words. Segmentation is explained to students as stretching words. Stretching is a more difficult skill for students than oral blending, so oral blending is taught first.

Oral Blending

A puppet named Maxwell is introduced into the curriculum when the students begin to blend words orally. Maxwell says words phoneme by phoneme. In other words, Maxwell stretches out words instead of saying them normally. Students are told they are helping Maxwell learn to speak normally. When teaching oral blending, move Maxwell's mouth as though he is the one talking. Students should watch Maxwell closely as he speaks.

In the oral-blending activities, say the words very slowly, emphasizing the individual sounds. The students say the words at a normal rate.

ACTIVITY AT A GLANCE

- Step 1: Introduce Maxwell to your students. Tell them he says words in a "funny" way. Ask your students to help you teach Maxwell to speak better by saying the fast way the words he says funny (or stretches).
- Step 2: Demonstrate how Maxwell talks by moving his mouth as you say a word slowly: */mmm/aaa/t/.*

- Step 3: Ask your students, **What word did Maxwell say?** On your cue, the students answer in unison, **mat.**
- Step 4: Repeat the procedure with the remaining words. Remember to correct all errors as they occur.
- Step 5: End with individual mastery check by having each student blend two or three words.

IN THE REAL WORLD

Sometimes students leave off a sound or invert sounds when they blend the sounds back into a whole word. Together with Maxwell, you can model the correct blending of the word. Maxwell then repeats the word in his stretched-out way, and the students get another chance to blend the word correctly.

Questions and Answers

Developing a personality for Maxwell as he interacts with the students can be a motivational tool for keeping the students engaged in the lesson.

Lesson 5

Activity 3
Oral Blending

Say the Word Game

(Use Maxwell the puppet to speak words in stretched form.)

Now we are going to play Say the Word. Remember, Maxwell can say words only in a funny way. Whenever he says a word, it is stretched. You have to tell me what word he said the fast way. I will do the first one.

My turn. *(Speak through Maxwell.)* /T/aaa/mmm/. *(Use the hand cues for stretching.)* What word did Maxwell say? *(Pause.)* **Tam.**

Do that one with me. Listen again as Maxwell stretches the word. When I cue, you tell me what word you heard. Listen. /T/aaa/mmm/. *(Pause.)* What word did you hear? *(Cue students. You may want to use the hand drop, open-palm cue.)* **Tam**

Right. Here's another one. Listen big. /Mmm/aaa/t/. What word? *(Cue students.)* **mat**

Repeat the process with the following words: sat, sit, tie, tea.

(Scaffold as necessary.)

Individual Practice

(Provide individual practice with 2–3 words per student.)

Very good. We have finished another activity. That means we can put a check mark on our lesson Mastery Sheet.

Language and Literacy Support for Oral Blending

In the oral blending activity that follows, you may provide additional vocabulary support and context to students as they learn to blend sounds to form words.

ACTIVITY AT A GLANCE

- Explain the meanings of vocabulary words, demonstrating when appropriate.
- Encourage students to discuss targeted vocabulary words, using the words in sentences and describing their meanings.
- Provide picture scaffolds to help students remember word meanings.

IN THE REAL WORLD

Although this section is designed for English-language learners, other students may also benefit from the additional vocabulary instruction and review, particularly students with intellectual disabilities, who typically experience language delays. Include vocabulary instruction for all students who need it, making sure that all students understand key vocabulary for the selection being read. When students understand the vocabulary, they can better comprehend the selection.

Questions and Answers

Activity 2
Oral Blending

Language and Literacy Support

During this activity we will be telling a story, and I want to be sure that you understand the words from the story.

The first word is *tortoise*. Who knows what a tortoise is? *(You may have to prompt further by saying:)* What do I mean if I say *A tortoise was crossing the road?* *(Accept reasonable responses.)*

That's right. A tortoise is like a turtle, but it lives only on land. Here is a picture of a tortoise. *(Hold up Pictures for Language and Literacy Support, page 13.)* A turtle lives partly on land and partly in water.

The next word is *hare.* The word *hare* has two meanings. The two meanings are spelled differently. We all know that *hair* is what we have on our heads.

There is another meaning for the word *hare.* What do I mean if I say *The hare was hopping across the field?* *(Accept reasonable responses.)*

133 Lesson 16

Yes. A hare is a wild rabbit with long ears. Here is a picture of a hare. *(Hold up Pictures for Language and Literacy Support, page 14.)*

The last word is *crawl.* Who knows what crawl means? *(You may have to prompt further by saying:)* What do I mean if I say *The baby crawls everywhere?* *(Accept reasonable responses.)*

Yes. Crawling is moving around on your hands and knees. Here is a picture of a baby crawling. *(Hold up Pictures for Language and Literacy Support, page 15.)*

Sometimes we say that things are crawling if they are moving very slowly. This is because, if you were crawling somewhere, it would take you a long time. You would be moving very slowly.

Good job!

(Take out Maxwell the puppet.)
Today Maxwell and I are going to tell you a story about a tortoise and a hare. Maxwell still stretches some words. He is going to need your help. Tell me what word he said.

(Get Maxwell ready to stretch words. If students say the word fast without prompting, you do not need to ask the question.)

Listen big. *(Pause.)* A hare boasted, *"No one is as /fff/aaa/sss/t/ as I am!"*
What did the hare say he was? fast

Yes. Good job saying the word the fast way! Let's continue. *The tortoise said, "I will /rrr/ aaa/sss/ you."*
What did the tortoise offer to do? race

"You slowpoke!" laughed the hare. "You will never /k/aaa/ch/ me!"
What did the hare say the tortoise couldn't do? catch the hare

The hare was off in a flash, while the tortoise had just begun to /k/rrr/aw/lll/ slowly along.
What did the tortoise do? crawl

The hare thought, "I am so far ahead that I will stop to /rrr/eee/sss/t/."
What did the hare decide to do? rest

When the hare awoke, the tortoise had /www/uuu/nnn/ the race.
What had the tortoise done? won the race

The embarrassed hare did not boast about his /sss/p/ eee/d/ ever again.
What didn't the hare boast about ever again? his speed

Excellent job listening and saying words the fast way. You helped Maxwell today! I will put a check mark on the Mastery Sheet.

Stretching Words

Stretching a word takes place only in the first few lessons. Segmenting is explained to students as "stretching" a word. A word is stretched so that each sound in the word can be heard. When stretching words, students stretch each sound and do not stop between sounds. Students should sound like they are humming the words. Continuous sounds are held two to three seconds. Stop sounds are said quickly.

For this format, you will say a word. Students then say the sounds in the word, holding up one finger for each sound. When students hold up a finger for each sound in a word, it creates a multisensory component that helps them to distinguish between sounds. You will guide the process by holding up a finger for each sound without saying the sounds yourself.

ACTIVITY AT A GLANCE

- Step 1: Tell your students they are going to stretch words. Remind them that they need to hold up one finger for each sound they hear in the word as they stretch it.
- Step 2: Say the word. **Am.** *(Pause.)* **Stretch *am.***
- Step 3: Cue students to begin stretching by holding up your index finger. Students say the word sound by sound, holding up one finger for each sound. Guide the process by holding up a finger for each sound without saying the sounds yourself.

- Step 4: Repeat the procedure with the remaining words. Correct all errors as they occur.
- Step 5: End with individual mastery check by having each student stretch one or two words.

IN THE REAL WORLD

Create a left-to-right orientation from the *student's* perspective for this activity. Use your right fist with the back of your hand facing your students. Raise your index finger for the first sound, then your middle finger, ring finger, and so on. This directionality helps students learn the left-to-right orientation necessary for reading text.

A common error students make is adding the short /u/ sound to the end of stop sounds. For example, the word bat should be stretched /b/aaa/t/ and not /buh/aaa/tuh/. By noticing this early, you can help your students make the sound correctly by modeling the correct pronunciation. Then have the students repeat the sound.

Questions and Answers

Lesson 5

Activity 4
Stretch the Word Game

Now you are going to play Stretch the Word. Remember, I will say a word, and you will tell me the sounds you hear in the word. Watch how I do it. First I hold up my fist. (Demonstrate.)

Next I slowly say each sound I hear in the word, and I hold up one finger as I say each sound.

My turn to do the first word. (pause) **Am.** (Pause.) I will stretch am. (Hold up one finger for each sound.) /Aaa/mmm/.

Now you stretch the word (pause) am (pause) with me. Hold up your fists.
Am. (Pause.) Stretch **am.**
(Teacher and students:) /aaa/mmm/

Excellent. Now by yourselves.
Am. (Pause.) **Stretch am. /aaa/mmm/**
(When students stretch by themselves, continue to use hand cues to guide them, but do not say anything.)

(Practice until all students can stretch am, following your finger cue as a group.)

Individual Practice

(Have each student stretch am.)

Here is a new word to stretch. We will do this one together. (Pause.)
At. Stretch **at.**
(Teacher and students:) /aaa/t/

(Scaffold as necessary.)

By yourselves. **At.** (Pause.) **Stretch at. /aaa/t/**

(Practice until all students can stretch at, following your finger cue as a group.)

Individual Practice

(Have each student stretch at.)

Here is another word to stretch. Let's see if you can do this one by yourselves the first time. Fists up.
Mat. (Pause.) Stretch **mat. /mmm/aaa/t/**

> Repeat the process with the following words: **sit, ram, rat.**

Individual Practice

(Check each student individually on 2 words.)

You have finished another part of the lesson. I will check off this activity on the lesson Mastery Sheet.

Stretch and Blend

After learning the separate skills of oral blending and stretching, your students will be required to combine the two skills into Stretch and Blend. These activities prepare students for sounding out written words and then blending them together in order to read them.

Maxwell the puppet is still a motivational tool. During Stretch and Blend activities, Maxwell is placed on the table. The students are told that Maxwell is still learning to speak normally, the fast way. Eventually Maxwell "graduates." He has learned to speak the fast way, and he says goodbye to the students.

ACTIVITY AT A GLANCE

- Step 1: Place Maxwell on the table.
- Step 2: Have students hold up their fists. Demonstrate by holding up your fist also.
- Step 3: Tell students to stretch the word. *Fat*. **Stretch *fat*.**
- Step 4: Cue students to begin stretching. Hold up one finger for each sound to guide the students. Do not say the sounds with the students.

- Step 5: Students say the word, one sound at a time, holding up one finger for each sound.
- Step 6: Ask the students, **What word did you stretch?** Cue students to answer.
- Step 7: Repeat the procedure with the remaining words. Correct all errors.
- Step 8: End with individual mastery check by having students stretch and blend one or two words.

IN THE REAL WORLD

It is important to give immediate corrective feedback to your students when they make an error. All errors should be corrected as soon as they occur. There are several types of errors students might make during stretch and/or blend activities:

- Saying the word slowly instead of fast.

- Saying the word fast instead of stretching it.

- Leaving out a sound (Teacher says */sss/aaa/t/;* students say */sss/aaa/*).

- Saying a different sound (Teacher says */sss/iii/t/;* students say */sss/eee/t/*).

- Adding an extra sound (Teacher says */sss/iii/t/;* students say */sss/iii/t/sss/*).

Use the error correction technique, Model-Lead-Test, to correct Stretch and Blend errors.

Questions and Answers

Activity 5
Stretch and Blend

(Place Maxwell the puppet or on *the table.)*
It is time to teach Maxwell to speak. First
I will say a word. Then you will stretch the
word, holding up one finger for each sound
you hear. Then say the word the fast way.

(Hold up your fist to demonstrate.)
Fists up. *(Pause.)* The first word is *fat.*
(Pause.) Stretch *fat. /fff/aaa/t/*
What word did you stretch? fat

Next word. *Fast.*
Stretch *fast. /fff/aaa/sss/t/*
What word did you stretch? fast

**Repeat the process with the following
words: fist, fit, fits, ramp.**

Individual Practice

(Provide individual practice.)

Excellent job stretching. You have earned
another check mark.

Phonemic Awareness (Teacher's Edition B)

The activities covered in Phonemic Awareness in **Teacher's Edition B** come from the same two categories of phonemic awareness skills previously introduced in **Teacher's Edition A:** Sound Discrimination and Segmentation and Blending.

FORMATS

- Sound Discrimination
  - Vowel Sounds
  - Short- and Long-Vowel Sounds
- Segmentation and Blending
  - Stretch and Blend

Starting in **Teacher's Edition B,** students will discriminate between the different vowel sounds within words. Students also learn to discriminate between the long- and short-vowel sounds. The terms "long vowel" and "short vowel" are never used in this program because they hold little meaning for students and can cause confusion for even high-achieving students. Instead, students learn that the set of five vowels sometimes say their sounds (short vowels) and sometimes say their names (long vowels).

In **Teacher's Edition B,** Stretch and Blend does not change in presentation format from the activities you have been practicing in **Teacher's Edition A.** However, the complexity of the words does change. Initially, the word types in the Stretch and Blend activities were simple: VC (at), CVC (mad), CVCC (milk). As the intervention progresses, the word types advance to CCVC (stop) and CCVCC (stand) and to the addition of word endings (stops, stopped, stopping). Stretch and Blend does not continue past **Teacher's Edition B.** Instead, the Stretch and Blend skill becomes embedded in spelling activities and in Sounding Out and Reading Fast activities.

Phonemic Awareness (Teacher's Edition B): Sound Discrimination

Vowel Discrimination

Vowel discrimination links auditory and visual skills. It does not occur until students have been taught the five short-vowel letter-sound correspondences.

For this activity, each student is given a set of vowel cards. The teacher says a word and asks students to hold up the card for the vowel sound they hear in each word.

ACTIVITY AT A GLANCE

- Step 1: Each student has a set of vowel cards arranged on the table in front of them: *a, e, i, o, u.*
- Step 2: Use your cards to review the vowel sounds one at a time. The students answer in unison as you hold up a card and say, This sound is /aaa/. **What sound?**
- Step 3: Say a word.
- Step 4: Students listen for the vowel sound in the word.

- Step 5: Cue students to hold up the card that stands for the sound they hear in the word.
- Step 6: Repeat the procedure with the remaining words. Correct all errors as they occur.
- Step 7: End with individual mastery check by giving each student two or three words.

IN THE REAL WORLD

Students sometimes have significant difficulty distinguishing between individual vowel sounds. When you first teach this activity, you may need to overemphasize the vowel sound as you say the word /mmm/ aaaaa/t/. The vowel sound can even be said a little louder than the consonant sounds. As students gain proficiency in identifying vowel sounds, you will no longer need to hold the vowel sound past the normal two to three seconds or to say it any louder than the consonant sounds in the word.

One or more students may hold up the wrong vowel card. Hold up the correct vowel card and say to the group, This sound is /aaa/; show me your card for the /aaa/ sound. Have the students say the vowel sound as they hold up the correct card. Back up one or two words, and begin the exercise again.

Consonant cards are also used to teach sound discrimination between the consonant sounds, /sh/, /ch/, and /th/.

Questions and Answers

Lesson 72

Activity 3
Letter-Sound Discrimination

Vowel Sounds

(Have ready the vowel cards from the Placement and Assessment Guide.)

Note: Follow this format: Pass out a set of vowel cards to each student. Each set contains cards for *a, e, i, o,* and *u.* Have students place all 5 vowel cards in front of them in order—*a, e, i, o, u.* Dictate words to students, and tap once for each word to cue students to hold up the correct vowel card for each word.

(After passing out the individual sets of vowel cards, use a set of cards to quickly review each vowel sound.)

(Hold up a, and say:) **What sound?** */aaa/*

Repeat the process with the remainder of the vowel cards.

Now I am going to say some words. For each word, listen for the vowel sound in that word. Next look for the card with the sound you just heard. When I tap, hold up the correct vowel sound for that word.

First word. *Fish.* *(Emphasize the vowel sound.)*

(Give students time to look for the correct card, and then tap.)

(Monitor to be sure students are holding the correct card.)

Repeat the process with the following words: box, tub, nest, skip, patch, bus, spot, step, sit.

Individual Practice

(Provide individual practice with 2–3 words per student.)

Great job identifying the vowel sounds. We have finished this activity. What should I do now?

243 Lesson 72

Vowel Discrimination: Listening for Long and Short *a*

When long vowels are introduced, students are taught that in some words the vowel says its name. Students then listen to words to determine if they hear the vowel sound or name. Remember, the terms "long vowel" and "short vowel" are not used with students because they do not convey meaning and can often lead to confusion.

ACTIVITY AT A GLANCE

- Step 1: Hold up Letter-Sound Card, and review: **What is this letter's sound? What is this letter's name?**
- Step 2: Say a word, emphasizing the vowel sound.
- Step 3: Ask students, **Did you hear** /aaa/ *(short /a/ sound)* or /āāā/ *(long /ā/ sound)* **in the word?**

- Step 4: On your cue, students say the sound they heard in the word.
- Step 5: Repeat the procedure with the remaining words.
- Step 6: End with individual mastery check.

IN THE REAL WORLD

It will help students having difficulty hearing the vowel sound if you overemphasize the vowel sound when you are pronouncing a word.

Students may give the vowel name instead of the vowel sound or the sound instead of the name. One method of correction is to build on a skill they have already mastered—stretching. Stretch the word, holding up one finger for each sound, tapping on the finger that is raised for the vowel, overemphasizing the sound. Finish stretching the word, and then, tapping again on the same finger, say, **What sound did you hear when I raised this finger?**

Use the Model-Lead-Test error-correction technique if students are still unable to distinguish between the vowel name and the vowel sound.

Questions and Answers

Phonemic Awareness (Teacher's Edition C)

By this time in the school year, most of the activities in the Phonemic Awareness Strand have faded. The skills have not. They are embedded within the other strands of the intervention curriculum. The remaining phonemic awareness activities continue to work on discriminating between long- and short-vowel sounds.

Lesson 77

Activity 1
Vowel Discrimination

Listening for Long and Short a

(Hold up the Aa letter-sound card.) What is this letter's sound? /aaa/

Good job. Remember that sometimes this letter also says its name. What is this letter's name? /āāā/

Now I am going to say some words. Tell me if you hear /aaa/ or /āāā/. Face. /Fff/ āāā /sss/. Did you hear /aaa/ or /āāā/ in face? /āāā/

> Repeat the process with the following words: **fat, wave, fad, fade, can, cane, cat, cake.**

(Scaffold, and correct as necessary. If students make an error, sound out the word again.)

Individual Practice

(Provide individual practice.)

Great job listening. We are off to a terrific start! I will mark the Mastery Sheet, so we can continue with our lesson.

279 Lesson 77

Strand Two: Letter-Sound Correspondences

SRA Early Interventions in Reading provides daily practice in reading and writing letter-sound correspondences. Letter-sound correspondence is taught by introducing one sound at a time. No more than three letter-sound correspondences are introduced each week.

When a new letter-sound correspondence is introduced, it is taught by letter-sound only so that students don't confuse the sound with the name of the letter. In this program, the most common or frequently occurring letter-sounds are introduced first. Letters that are visually similar or that sound alike are separated by at least three other letter-sound introductions so that students can more easily distinguish them.

The teacher carefully models and monitors accurate pronunciation of letter-sound correspondences. Continuous sounds are held or hummed two to three seconds. Stop sounds are not held; otherwise, they become distorted.

Letter-Sound Correspondences (Teacher's Edition A)

The Letter-Sound Correspondences activities in **Teacher's Edition A** come from three categories of letter-sound correspondence skills: Letter-Sound Introduction, Letter-Sound Review, and Letter-Sound Dictation. These skills are discussed here more fully in the order in which they are introduced in the intervention.

FORMATS

- Letter-Sound Introduction
  —Writing the Sound
- Letter-Sound Review
- Letter-Sound Dictation

The introductory format, Letter-Sound Introduction, is used the first time a letter-sound correspondence is presented. During this activity students learn to associate the sounds with letters, as well as how to write the letter.

Once a letter-sound correspondence has been taught, it will be reviewed frequently. This review occurs through two formats— Letter-Sound Review and Letter-Sound Dictation. At least one of these two activities takes place in each lesson.

Letter-sound cards are used to introduce letter-sound correspondences and to correct student errors in writing exercises, Letter-Sound Dictation, and Stretch and Spell.

m
■mb

1 Monkey

a

2 Lamb

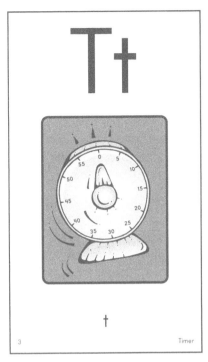

t

3 Timer

s
ce
ci_

4 Sausages

r
wr_

5 Robot

Letter-Sound Correspondences (Teacher's Edition A): Letter-Sound Introduction

Introducing Letter-Sounds

Each sound is introduced with a letter-sound card that helps students associate letters with sounds. For example, the /mmm/ sound is introduced with a picture of Muzzy the Monkey.

The first time you introduce a letter-sound correspondence, hold up the card for the letter-sound, model the sound of the letter, and ask the students to say the sound. At this time, check to make sure students are pronouncing the sounds correctly. For many of the sounds, a short poem is then read while students listen for words that have the new sound. Afterward students practice tracing and writing the new letter.

When a new letter-sound correspondence is introduced, it becomes part of a cumulative letter review. In cumulative practice, students read letter-sound correspondences they learned in previous lessons.

Make sure alternate spellings on letter-sound cards that have not been introduced are covered. Students should see only those letters and letter-combinations that already have been introduced.

ACTIVITY AT A GLANCE

- Step 1: Hold up a letter-sound card and say, **This letter's sound is _____.** Have students say the sound first with you and then on their own. Check for mastery by giving each student a turn to read the letter-sound.

- Step 2: Read the accompanying poem, which appears both in the **Teacher's Edition** and on the back of the card, and have students listen for words that have the sound. Ask the students, **What words did you hear with the _____ sound in them?**

- Step 3: Hold up the letter-sound card again, and review the sound. Point to the lowercase letter and say, **Everybody, what is this letter's sound?** Then repeat with the uppercase letter.

- Step 4: Build individual mastery by having each student read the new sound.

IN THE REAL WORLD

Students enjoy listening to the short poems. In every poem students will be asked to repeat a sound with you. Example: **Can you help Carlos take pictures with his camera? /k/ /k/ /k/.** For this poem, you can add a fun element by putting your hands by your eyes and pretending to take a picture as you make the sound. The students usually join in. Being playful with the students can help keep up their energy. Keep it brief, and don't let it slow the pace.

Sometimes students are not able to tell you a word that begins with the target sound.

Repeat the sound you want students to listen for. Ask them to listen carefully for words that contain that sound as you reread one line from the story. Emphasize the sound you want them to hear.

After introducing the letter-sound correspondence, place the letter-sound card somewhere students can see it and you can reference it throughout the activity.

Questions and Answers

Lesson 15

Activity 2
Letter-Sound Introduction

Language and Literacy Support (ELD)

During this activity, we will be reading a poem, and I want to make sure you understand the words from the poem. The first word is *fan*. Who knows what fan means? *(You may have to prompt students further by saying:)* What do I mean if I say *We turned on the fan*? *(Accept reasonable responses.)* That's right. A fan blows air to cool you off. *(Demonstrate by fanning yourself.)* Here is a picture of a fan. *(Show Ff Letter-Sound Card.)*

The next word is *fox*. Does anyone know what a fox is? *(You may have to prompt students further by saying:)* What do I mean if I say *There was a fox outside the chicken pen*? *(Accept reasonable responses.)* Yes. A fox is a small wild animal a little like a wolf or a dog but smaller, with shorter legs. Foxes have large ears and bushy tails. Here is a picture of a fox. *(Hold up Pictures for Language and Literacy Support, page 12.)*

The last word is *whir*. Does anyone know what whir means? *(You may have to prompt*

students further by saying:) What do I mean if I say *Fans whir in windows on hot summer days*? *(Accept reasonable responses.)* Yes. Whir is a quiet sound. An electric fan makes a whirring sound. Whirring sounds like this. *(Demonstrate by rolling your tongue.)* Good job.

(Hold up the Ff letter-sound card.) This letter's sound is /fff/. Say it with me. *(Teacher and students:)* /fff/ Again. Say it with me. *(Teacher and students:)* /fff/ Your turn. What sound? /fff/

Individual Practice

(Ask each student individually.)

Good job. I am going to read a poem about Franny the Fan. Listen. I will stretch the beginning of the word *Franny*. /Fff/ranny. What is the beginning sound you hear in the word /Fff/ranny? /fff/ Yes. The beginning sound in *Franny* is /fff/. Good listening. Listen again as I stretch the beginning of the word *fan*. /Fff/an. What is the beginning sound you hear in the word /fff/an? /fff/ That is right, so we know *(point to f)* this is the first letter we hear in *Franny* and *fan*. Here is a poem about Franny the Fan. This poem has many words with the /fff/ sound.

Listen big so you can hear them. I'll ask you about them after I read the poem. *(Read the poem, emphasizing the /fff/ /fff/ /fff/ sounds. Hold each individual sound 2 seconds.)*

/fff/ /fff/ /fff/ /fff/ /fff/ — What's that funny sound?
It's Franny the Fan going round and round.
And this is the sound that old fan makes:
/fff/ /fff/ /fff/ /fff/ /fff/.
When it gets too hot, you see,
Franny cools the family: /fff/ /fff/ /fff/ /fff/ /fff/.
She fans Father's face,
And Foxy's fur,
And Felicity's feet.
Hear the fan whir: /fff/ /fff/ /fff/ /fff/ /fff/.
Can you make Franny the Fan go fast? *(Have students say quickly:)* /fff/ /fff/ /fff/ /fff/ /fff/
Faster? /fff/ /fff/ /fff/ /fff/ /fff/
Fastest? /fff/ /fff/ /fff/ /fff/ /fff/
What words did you hear with the /fff/ sound? *(Discuss.)*

(Hold up the Ff letter-sound card. Point to f.) Everybody, what is this letter's sound? /fff/ *(Point to F.)* What is this letter's sound? /fff/ *(Put the letter-sound card on the table for students to see.)* Here is a picture of Franny the Fan. She is here to remind you of this letter's sound. Great job saying /fff/. What should I do now? *(Encourage students to tell you to check off the activity on the Mastery Sheet.)*

Writing Letter-Sounds

After introducing a letter-sound correspondence, model writing the new letter-sound correspondence, describing each stroke as you make it. Use the letter formation guide in the Appendix of each **Teacher's Edition** as a reference.

Then have students trace the letter while you talk them through each pencil stroke.

Students say the sound as they trace and write the sound. Saying the sound while they are writing the corresponding letter or letters is a preliminary step toward successful spelling.

Require students to write as neatly and as quickly as they can. Pace the students in this way: **Every time I say the sound, you write the letter for that sound.**

ACTIVITY AT A GLANCE

- Step 1: Hold up the letter-sound card, and review the sound with your students.
- Step 2: Pass out pencils, and have students turn to the correct activity page. Direct students to the section on the activity sheet where they will trace and write the letter.
- Step 3: Using the marker board, model writing the new letter-sound correspondence, describing each stroke you make.

- Step 4: Students practice tracing and writing the new sound as you monitor closely for individual mastery. Students say the sound each time they trace and write the letter-sound.

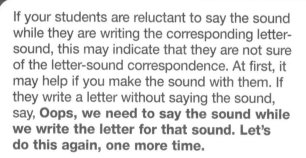

IN THE REAL WORLD

If your students are reluctant to say the sound while they are writing the corresponding letter-sound, this may indicate that they are not sure of the letter-sound correspondence. At first, it may help if you make the sound with them. If they write a letter without saying the sound, say, **Oops, we need to say the sound while we write the letter for that sound. Let's do this again, one more time.**

Monitor your students closely while they are writing the letter. Stop them as soon as an error in writing begins to occur so that they don't practice an incorrect way of writing a letter. Model the letter for them again on the marker board, and then have them rewrite the letter.

Questions and Answers

Lesson 15

Activity 6
Writing the Letter

(Have the Ff letter-sound card ready. Have students open their activity books to page 19. Allow no more than 4 seconds to write each letter.)

(Hold up the Ff letter-sound card. Point to f.)

What is this letter's sound? /fff/

Now we are going to learn how to write the letter that stands for the /fff/ sound. Watch how I write it. *(Model, explaining each stroke you make. Use the letter formation guide at the back of this book.)*

On the activity sheet, the letters are almost finished. Put your pencil on the big dot of the first letter. *(Demonstrate, and monitor.)*

Let's trace that letter together. *(Walk students through each pencil stroke. Have students say the /f/ sound as they trace the letter and write it on their own in this activity.)*

Good job tracing the letter that says /fff/. Trace the next letter fast. Trace it by yourselves.
(Monitor, and correct as necessary.)

(Have students trace all the f's on the first line.)

Good job tracing the letter that says /fff/. Now let's write the letter that stands for the /fff/ sound. Touch the big dot of the first letter, and trace it. Say the /fff/ sound as you neatly write the letter f.

(Have students complete all the f's on the second line.)

Good job writing the letter that says /fff/. Now you are going to write the letter that says /fff/ by yourselves. Write the letter three times. *(Point to the line on which students will write their f's. Remind students to softly say the /fff/ sound as they write the letters.)*
(Monitor, and correct as necessary.)

Excellent job writing the letter that makes the /fff/ sound. Now we are going to write two words. Look at the words underneath your line of f's. Put your finger on the first word. Let's sound it out together.
(Teacher and students:) **/fff/aaa/nnn/**
Read it. fan

Write the word fan on the line. *(Have students say the sounds as they write the letters.)*
(Monitor, and correct as necessary.)

Repeat the process with the word fat.

Good job writing words with the /fff/ sound. I will put a check mark on the Mastery Sheet so we can go to the next activity.

Name

Lesson 15

f

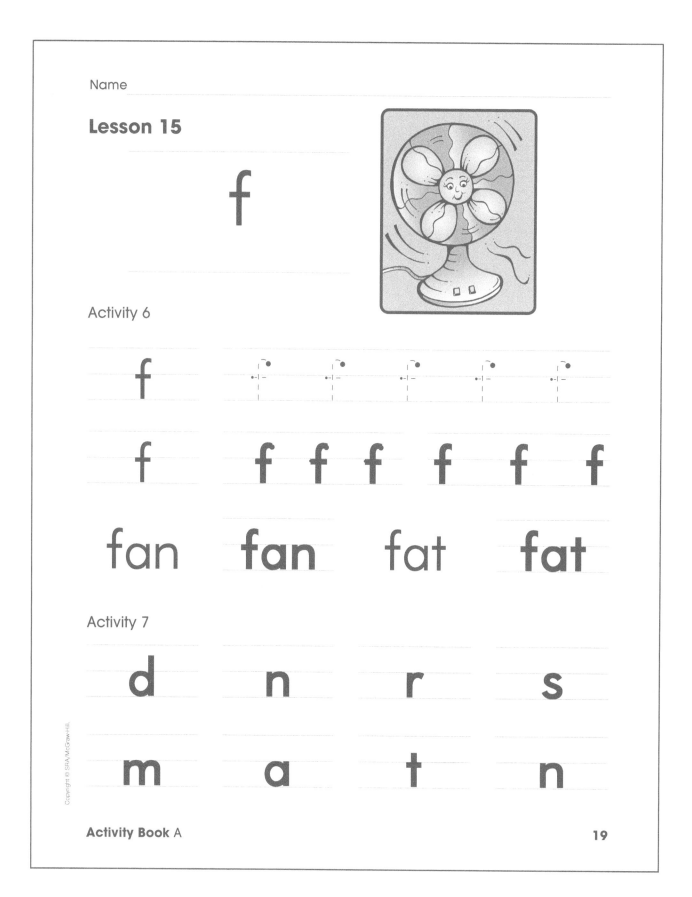

Activity 6

f

f f f f f f f

f

fan fan fat fat

Activity 7

d   n   r   s

m   a   t   n

Letter Formation: Writing Letters

The main purpose of writing exercises is to reinforce the letter-to-sound correspondence. This is why students should say the sound while they write the sound. Practice in writing letter-sound correspondences is foundational to the Stretch and Spell activities in the Word Recognition and Spelling Strand, where students write whole words based on the letter-sounds they have learned.

Writing exercises should not turn into handwriting lessons. It is important to keep up the pace and to encourage your students to write as accurately and quickly as they can with no erasing. A letter formation guide is provided in the Appendix of each **Teacher's Edition,** but you may also choose to use the writing system specific to your school.

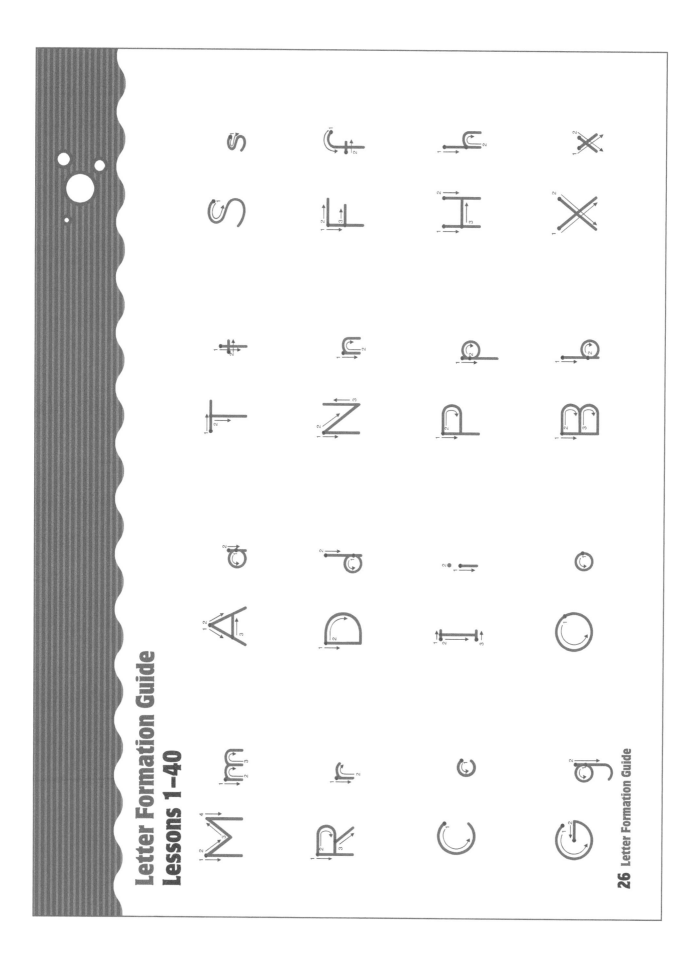

Letter Formation Guide
Lessons 1–40

Staff Development Guide, Level 1

26 Letter Formation Guide

Letter-Sound Correspondences (Teacher's Edition A): Letter-Sound Review

After a letter-sound correspondence is introduced, it is added to a cumulative letter-sound review. During Letter-Sound Review activities, use the point-touch cue. Focus student attention on the letter by pointing to it. Then, touch under the letter to cue students to read it. Touch under continuous sounds for about two seconds before lifting your finger and pointing to the next letter. Tell students to hold the sound for as long as you touch under the letter-sound. For stop sounds, point-touch, and lift your finger quickly. If you do not lift quickly, students will distort the sound by adding a *schwa* sound; /t/ will become /*tuh*/.

At first, there are directional arrows and dots under letters as another visual cue. The arrows and dots gradually fade. Dots reappear occasionally under a letter-sound represented by a letter combination so students know to read the letter combination as one sound.

ACTIVITY AT A GLANCE

- Step 1: Hold up the letter-sound card of the last letter-sound correspondence introduced. Review the sound for that letter with your students. **What is this letter-sound?**

- Step 2: Hold the **Teacher's Edition** at shoulder level so all students can easily see the page of letter-sounds. Tell students, **When I touch under a letter-sound, say its sound. Keep saying its sound for as long as I touch under it.**

- Step 3: Touch under each letter-sound. Hold your finger under continuous sounds for two to four seconds. Touch under stop sounds only briefly to emphasize that they are said quickly.

- Step 4: End with individual mastery check by having each student read three or four letter-sounds.

IN THE REAL WORLD

Correct errors by pointing to the letter-sound that was mispronounced and say, **This letter's sound is _____.** Say the correct sound for students. Ask your students to repeat the sound. **What sound is this?** Then back up two or three letters, and begin again.

Create a gamelike quality by varying the time you hold under a continuous sound during letter-sound review. This reinforces the idea that the students are supposed to hold the sound as long as you touch under it. Add a fun element by holding under the occasional continuous sound for three or four seconds, letting your eyes get big as if you know students are running out of air, and then quickly move to the next sound. Always remember to touch under a continuous sound for two or three seconds and to move quickly off stop sounds. Never hold a stop sound, or the sound will be distorted.

Questions and Answers . . . .

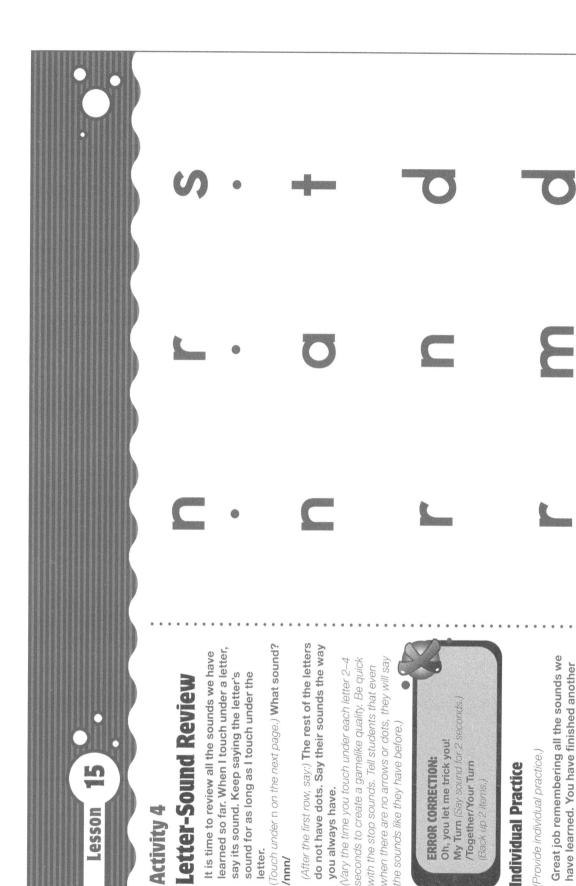

n	r
s	.
.	n
t	a
d	n
r	m
d	r

Activity 4
Letter-Sound Review

It is time to review all the sounds we have learned so far. When I touch under a letter, say its sound. Keep saying the letter's sound for as long as I touch under the letter.

(Touch under n on the next page.) **What sound?** **/nnn/**

(After the first row, say:) **The rest of the letters do not have dots. Say their sounds the way you always have.**

(Vary the time you touch under each letter 2–4 seconds to create a gamelike quality. Be quick with the stop sounds. Tell students that even when there are no arrows or dots, they will say the sounds like they have before.)

ERROR CORRECTION:
Oh, you let me trick you!
My Turn *(Say sound for 2 seconds.)*
/Together/Your Turn
(Back up 2 items.)

Individual Practice

(Provide individual practice.)

Great job remembering all the sounds we have learned. You have finished another activity perfectly. I will put a check mark on the lesson Mastery Sheet.

126 Lesson 15

Arrows and Dots

In letter-sound review, students read each letter-sound as you touch under it. Initially, arrows and dots appear under the letters as an added visual cue. The arrows promote left-to-right directionality. Dots are used to differentiate sounds. The use of dots and arrows also helps students make the transition from reading individual sounds to sounding out words and reading connected text. After a few lessons, arrows and dots gradually begin to fade. Dots temporarily reappear throughout the lessons for certain sounds that are represented by letter combinations or to help students remember to read doubled letters as one sound. Below is a description of the progression of the curriculum from arrows and dots under letter-sounds to instances with no arrows or dots under the letter-sounds for the Letter-Sound Correspondences Strand.

1. Letter-sounds first appear in the intervention with arrows and dots under each letter-sound.

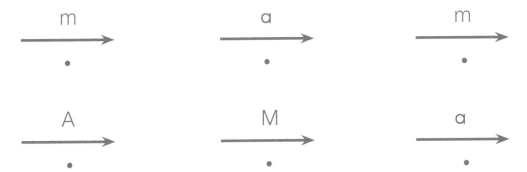

2. Starting in Lesson 9, the arrows begin to fade.

3. In Lesson 14, the dots begin to fade. Dots will reappear from time to time for letter combinations that form one letter-sound and for doubled letters as a cue to students that the letters form one sound.

Letter-Sound Correspondences (Teacher's Edition A): Letter-Sound Dictation

Letter-Sound Dictation is a variant of cumulative letter-sound review in which students practice writing letters for sounds they have learned. Letter-Sound Dictation requires students to retrieve information, a more advanced skill than simple recognition.

ACTIVITY AT A GLANCE

- Step 1: Pass out pencils, and have students turn to the correct activity page.
- Step 2: Say to the students, **When I say a sound, write its letter the small way. Write it as fast and as neatly as you can. Remember to say the sound while you write the letter.**
- Step 3: Dictate one sound at a time. Hold continuous sounds two seconds. Do not hold stop sounds.
- Step 4: Students say the sound as they write each letter. Check for individual mastery by monitoring students closely while they are writing the letter. If students make an error, stop them, model the letter on the board, and have students rewrite the letter correctly.

IN THE REAL WORLD

You want your students to write neatly, with no erasing, but as fast as they can.

Your students are continually reinforcing letter-sound correspondence by saying the sound each time they write the corresponding letter. Listen carefully to make sure that the sound they say matches the letter they are writing. **You said /b/, but you wrote /d/.** Have them repeat the correct sound, and then have them write the correct letter while they say its sound.

Questions and Answers

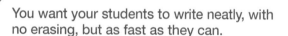

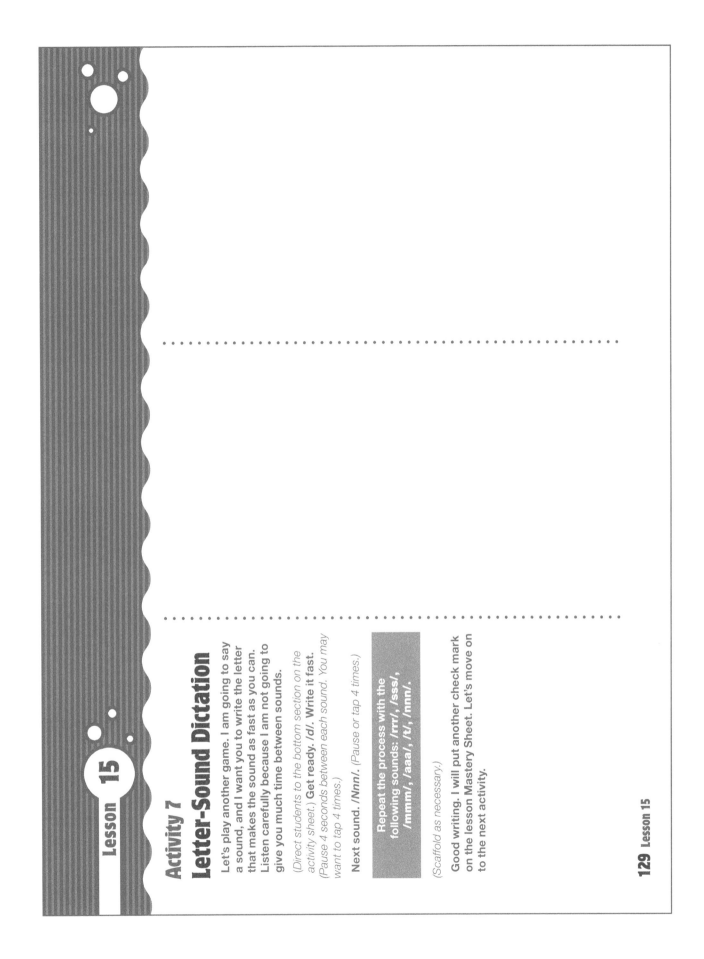

Lesson 15

Activity 7
Letter-Sound Dictation

Let's play another game. I am going to say a sound, and I want you to write the letter that makes the sound as fast as you can. Listen carefully because I am not going to give you much time between sounds.

(Direct students to the bottom section on the activity sheet.) **Get ready.** */d/.* **Write it fast.** *(Pause 4 seconds between each sound. You may want to tap 4 times.)*

Next sound. */Nnn/.* *(Pause or tap 4 times.)*

Repeat the process with the following sounds: */rrr/, /sss/, /mmm/, /aaa/, /t/, /nnn/.*

(Scaffold as necessary.)

Good writing. I will put another check mark on the lesson Mastery Sheet. Let's move on to the next activity.

129 Lesson 15

Name _____

Lesson 15

f

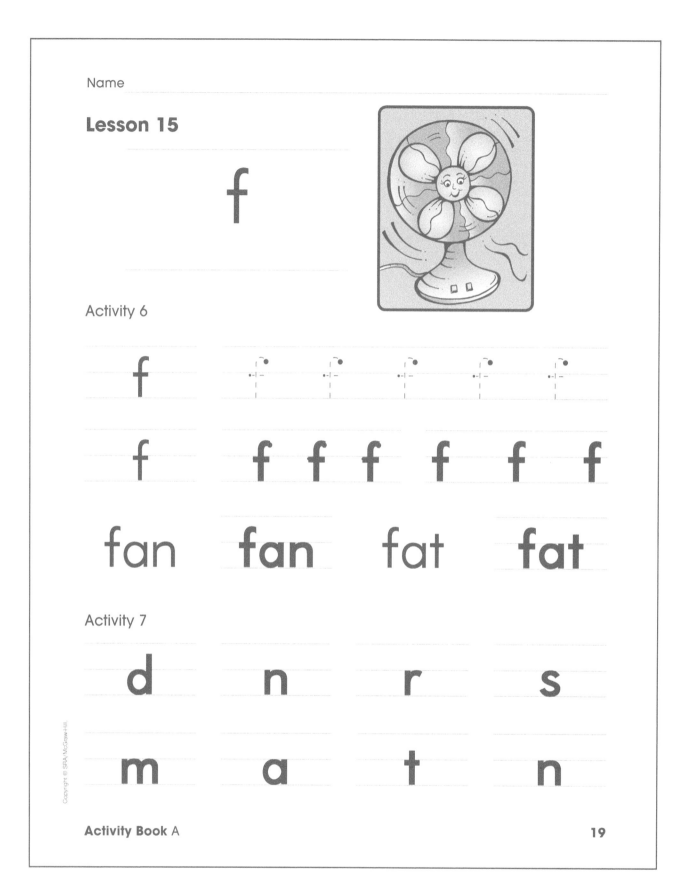

Activity 6

f

f   f   f   f   f   f   f

fan   **fan**   fat   **fat**

Activity 7

d   n   r   s

m   a   t   n

Letter-Sound Correspondences (Teacher's Edition A): Letter-Sound Introduction

Introducing Variant Spellings

Starting with Lesson 35, students learn that some sounds can be written more than one way. Hold up the letter-sound card and review the previously introduced spelling. Uncover the variant spelling on the letter-sound card, and tell students that the sound can be spelled more than one way.

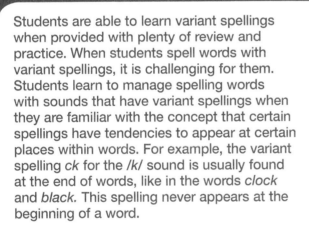

ACTIVITY AT A GLANCE

- Step 1: Hold up the letter-sound card, and review the previously introduced spelling.
- Step 2: Uncover the variant spelling, and introduce it.
- Step 3: Tell students if the spelling appears more often in a certain position within a word. For instance, the *ck* spelling for the /k/ sound never appears at the beginning of a word.

- Step 4: Read the poem for the letter-sound, having your students identify words with the target sound. Continue the normal procedure for introducing new letter-sound correspondences.
- Step 5: Review the new spelling for the sound with your students: **Everybody, what sound?** (and, if applicable) **Where do we usually find this spelling in the word?**
- Step 6: End with individual mastery check by having each student read both representations of the sound from the letter-sound card.

IN THE REAL WORLD

Students are able to learn variant spellings when provided with plenty of review and practice. When students spell words with variant spellings, it is challenging for them. Students learn to manage spelling words with sounds that have variant spellings when they are familiar with the concept that certain spellings have tendencies to appear at certain places within words. For example, the variant spelling *ck* for the /k/ sound is usually found at the end of words, like in the words *clock* and *black.* This spelling never appears at the beginning of a word.

Review and practice for writing alternate spellings are provided in Letter-Sound Review and Letter-Sound Dictation activities. Automatic recognition of alternate spellings will help the students with advanced activities such as Sounding Out and Stretch and Spell.

Questions and Answers . . . .

Activity 1
Letter-Sound Introduction

ELD

Language and Literacy Support

During this activity we will be reading a poem, and I want to make sure you understand all the words from the poem.

The first word is pack. Who knows what a pack is? *(If students give another correct meaning, acknowledge it, but focus on the contextual meaning in the poem.)*

(You may have to prompt students further by saying:) **Here is a hint. She carried her books in her pack.** *(Accept reasonable responses.)*

That is right. Pack is a short way to say "backpack." Here is a picture of a pack. *(Hold up Pictures for Language and Literacy Support, page 34.)*

The next word is tack. Does anyone know what a tack is?

(You may have to prompt students further by saying:) **What do I mean if I say The teacher put the sign on the wall with a tack?** *(Accept reasonable responses.)*

Yes. A tack is a small, sharp-pointed nail. Here is a picture of a tack. *(Hold up Pictures for Language and Literacy Support, page 35.)*

Good job!

(Hold up the Cc letter-sound card.)

This letter's sound is /k/. Say it with me.
(Teacher and students:) **/k/**
Again. Say it with me.
(Teacher and students:) **/k/**
Your turn. What sound? /k/

Individual Practice

(Ask each student individually.)

(Point to ck on the letter-sound card.)

Sometimes the /k/ sound is spelled with the letters ck, but it is never written this way at the beginning of words.

I am going to read a poem about Mack and his pack. Listen. I will stress the end of the word Mack. Ma *(pause)* **/k/.**
What is the ending sound you hear in the word Ma *(pause)* **/k/? /k/**

Yes. The ending sound in Mack is /k/. Good listening. Listen again as I stress the end of the word pack. Pa *(pause)* **/k/.**
What is the ending sound you hear in the word pa *(pause)* **/k/? /k/**

Yes. So we know *(point to ck)* **these letters make the last sound we hear in Mack and pack. Here is a poem about Mack. This poem has many words with the /k/ sound in them. Listen big so you hear them. I will ask you about them after I read the poem.**

(Read the poem, emphasizing the /k/ /k/ /k/ sounds. Have students say the /k/ /k/ /k/ sounds with you.)

There once was a boy named Mack.
Everywhere he went, he carried his pack on his back.
When he walked, his pack went /k/ /k/ /k/.

Mack liked to collect things and put them into his pack.
One day while he was walking, he found a sock, a rock, a tack, and a clock!
He put them into his pack, and it went /k/ /k/ /k/.

Lesson 35

One rainy day Mack was feeling sick.
He didn't feel like he could pick up even the tiniest stick.
So he listened to the clock and heard it go tick-tock.
Then, as he took off his pack, it went /k/ /k/ /k/.

"Oh, well," thought Mack,
"Tomorrow's another day.
I will be back to filling my pack."

And what sound do you think his pack will make?
(Have students say:) **/k/ /k/ /k/**

What words with the /k/ sound did you hear? *(Discuss.)*

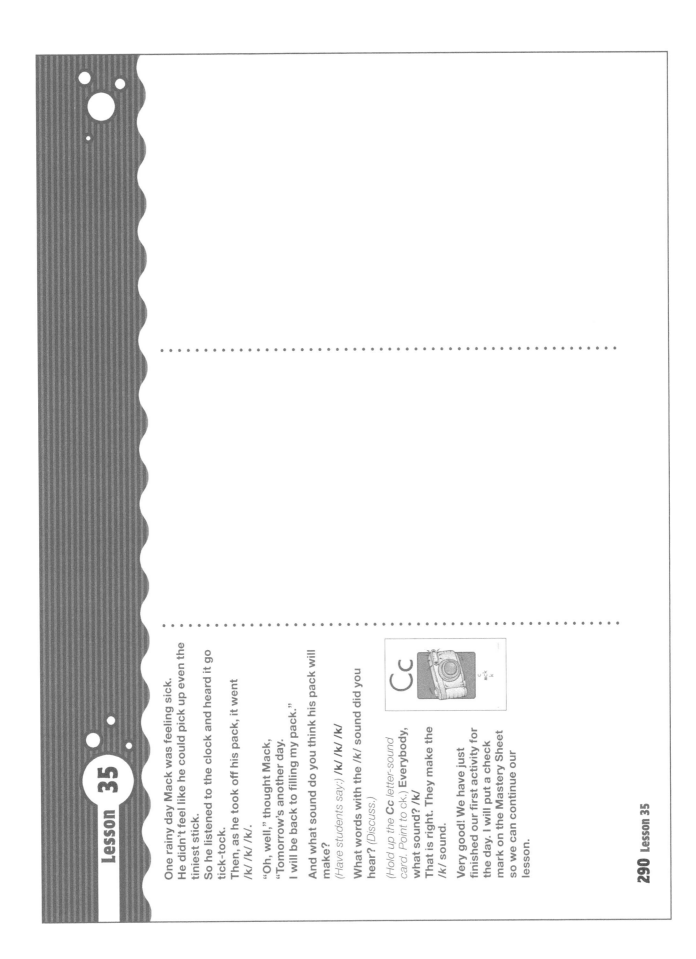

*(Hold up the **Cc** letter-sound card. Point to* ck.*)* **Everybody, what sound?** **/k/**
That is right. They make the /k/ sound.

Very good! We have just finished our first activity for the day. I will put a check mark on the Mastery Sheet so we can continue our lesson.

290 Lesson 35

Letter-Sound Correspondences (Teacher's Edition B)

The Letter-Sound Correspondence activities presented in **Teacher's Edition B** come from the same three categories of Letter-Sound Correspondence skills previously introduced in **Teacher's Edition A:** Letter-Sound Introduction, Letter-Sound Review, and Letter-Sound Dictation. As letter-sound correspondences continue to be introduced, students practice reading letters that can be read more than one way and writing sounds that can be written more than one way.

FORMATS

- Letter-Sound Introduction
    Writing the Sound
- Letter-Sound Review
- Letter-Sound Dictation

Letter-Sound Correspondences (Teacher's Edition B): Letter-Sound Introduction

Letters with Multiple Sounds

In **Teacher's Edition B,** students learn how to read a sound one way and then another way. For example, the /th/ sound can be voiced as in the word *them* or unvoiced as in the word *bath.* Your students need to know that when they sound out a word and it is not quite recognizable, they may need to "flex" the sound by trying it one way and then another until the word makes sense.

When introducing the new way to read /th/, have students put their hands on their throats to feel the difference between the two sounds. The voiced /th/, as in *them,* vibrates in the throat. The unvoiced /th/, as in *bath,* does not.

Hold up the letter-sound card and remind students of the sound already associated with the letter-sound correspondence by having them say the sound. Point to the letter-sound and say there is another way to read this letter-sound. Say the new sound. Have students say the sound first with you and then by themselves. Continue with the normal procedure for introducing letter-sound correspondences. At the end of the lesson, ask students, **What is one sound these letters make? Now, what is the other sound these letters make?**

ACTIVITY AT A GLANCE

- Step 1: Hold up the letter-sound card, and remind students of the sound they have already associated with the letter-sound.
- Step 2: Tell students these letters make another sound. Say the sound.
- Step 3: Have students say the sound first with you and then by themselves.
- Step 4: If provided, read the poem with the new sound in it for your students to identify, continuing the normal procedure for introducing new letter-sound correspondences.

- Step 5: Review both sounds with your students. **Everybody, what is one sound these letters make? What is another sound they make?**
- Step 6: End with individual mastery check by having each student read the letter-sound both ways they know.

IN THE REAL WORLD

Students who are having trouble pronouncing sounds may benefit from having you describe where and how the sound is formed in the mouth. If a student is having trouble pronouncing the /th/ sound, tell him or her to put the tip of the tongue between the teeth to make this sound. Model this for the student.

Questions and Answers . . . .

Activity 3
Part A: Letter-Sound Introduction

ELD

Language and Literacy Support

During this activity we will be reading a poem about Theo the Thimble, and I want to make sure you know all the words.

The first word is *thimble*. Who knows what a thimble is?

(You may need to prompt further by saying:) **What do I mean if I say** *My mother used a thimble while she sewed the dress so that she wouldn't hurt her finger with the needle?* *(Accept reasonable responses.)*

That's right! A thimble is a small cap that goes over your finger to protect it while you are sewing. *(Hold up Pictures for Language and Literacy Support, page 60.)*

The next word is *rubs*. Who knows what *rubs* means?

(You may need to prompt further by saying:) **What do I mean if I say** *She rubs her hands to warm them up when they are cold?* *(Accept reasonable responses.)*

Yes. You rub something by pressing two things together and moving them back and forth. *(Demonstrate with two items or your hands.)*

The last word is *thunder*. Who remembers what thunder is? *(Accept reasonable responses.)*

That's right. Thunder is the noise that comes right after lightning during a storm.

Nice job!

(Write th on the marker board.) One sound these letters make is /th/ as in the words *this, those,* and *them*. *(This is called the voiced sound of th.)*

(Hold up the unvoiced th letter-sound card.)

These letters have another sound. You already know the /th/ (voiced) sound. Now we are going to learn the other sound. The other sound these two letters make is /th/ (unvoiced) as in the words *think* and *thin*.

Say it with me. /th/

(Teacher and students:) /th/ (unvoiced)

Again. Say it with me. /th/

(Teacher and students:) /th/

Your turn. /th/

What is the other sound these letters make? /th/ (voiced)

Individual Practice

(Ask each student individually.)

Good job. I am going to read a poem about Theo the Thimble. Listen.

I will stretch the beginning of *Theo*. /Th/ (pause) eo.

What sound do you hear at the beginning of the word /Th/ (pause) eo? /th/

Good listening. Now listen again as I stretch the beginning of the word *thimble*. /Th/ (pause) imble.

What sound do you hear at the beginning of the word /th/ (pause) imble? /th/

Yes. So we know these *(point to the unvoiced th letter-sound card)* are the letters we hear at the beginning of the words Theo and thimble.

Here is a poem about Theo the Thimble. This poem has many words with the /th/ sound. Listen big so you can hear them. I will ask you about them after I read the poem.

(Read the poem, emphasizing the /th/ sound. Have students say /th/ /th/ /th/ with you.)

Theo Thimble is a thinker.
Theo thinks and thinks and thinks.
And when he thinks, he rubs his head.
/th/ /th/ /th/ /th/ /th/

Theo thinks of many things—
Thin things,
Thick things,
All different kinds of things.
/th/ /th/ /th/ /th/ /th/

Theo thinks of thunder—
Loud thunder,
Soft thunder,
All different types of thunder.
/th/ /th/ /th/ /th/ /th/

Thin things, thick things,
Loud thunder, soft thunder—
The thoughts Theo thinks.
/th/ /th/ /th/ /th/ /th/

What words with the /th/ sound did you hear? (Discuss.)

(Hold up the unvoiced **th** letter-sound card. Point to th.)

Everybody, what is one sound these letters make? (The voiced sound as in these and them.) /**th**/

What is the other sound these letters make? (The unvoiced sound as in thin and think.) /**th**/

(Place the unvoiced **th** letter-sound card on the table where all students can see it.)

Here is a picture of Theo the Thimble. He is here to remind you of the /th/ sound.

Part B: Thumbs Up— Thumbs Down Game

Beginning and Ending Sounds

Now you know two different ways the letters *th* can sound: /*th*/ as in *this* and /*th*/ as in *thimble*. We are going to play the Thumbs Up—Thumbs Down Game. When I say a word, give a thumbs-up if you hear /*th*/ as in *thimble*. Put your thumbs up *only* if you hear /*th*/ as in *thimble*. If the word does not have /*th*/ as in *thimble* in it, put your thumbs down.

Get ready. Listen big. First word. *Up.* **Does *up* have the /*th*/ sound at the beginning?** No.

So will you give a thumbs-up? No. **Show me.** (Students should give a thumbs-down.)

(Monitor, and correct as necessary.)

Good job. Next word. *Thumb.*

Repeat the process with the following words: **thump,** *this*, **thimble, tap, think, motor, thanks.**

*Students may have difficulty hearing the difference with the voiced /*th*/ as in *this.* If students make an error, go back, and sound out the word together.

Now I am going to say some more words. When I say a word, put your thumbs up if the word ends with /*th*/ (*unvoiced*). If the word does not end with /*th*/, put your thumbs down.

Get ready to listen. First word. *With.* (Students should give a thumbs-up.)

(Monitor, and correct as necessary.)

Good job. Let's continue.

Repeat the process with the following words: **push, beneath, path, math, ask, teeth, bath, feet.**

Great job hearing the /*th*/ sound in words. I will mark the Mastery Sheet.

Letter-Sound Correspondence (Teacher's Edition B): Letter-Sound Review

Cumulative Practice: Multiple Spellings of the Same Sound and Letters that Can Be Read More Than One Way

As students progress through the program, daily, cumulative letter-sound review will include sounds that are spelled more than one way, such as /k/, represented by c, ck, and k, and letters that can be pronounced more than one way, such as /th/, both voiced and unvoiced.

During cumulative letter review, students will practice lists that have one sound represented several ways. These items are treated like all other items using the point-touch cue.

Letters that represent more than one sound are trickier. When you touch under a letter that can be read more than one way, ask, **What is one way to read this sound?** After students answer, ask, **What is another way to read this sound?** If they are unable to remember the alternate sound, treat it as an error. Tell students the sound, and then back up two or three letters and begin again.

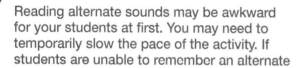

ACTIVITY AT A GLANCE

- Step 1: Begin the activity as you have in **Teacher's Edition A: Now it is time to review letter-sounds you have learned so far. When I touch under a letter-sound, tell me its sound. Keep saying its sound until I touch under the next letter-sound.**

- Step 2: When you reach a sound that can be read more than one way, touch under the letter-sound and say, **First sound.** After students respond, touch under the letter-sound again, and say, **Second sound.**

- Step 3: End with individual mastery check by having each student read three or four sounds.

IN THE REAL WORLD

Reading alternate sounds may be awkward for your students at first. You may need to temporarily slow the pace of the activity. If students are unable to remember an alternate sound, treat it as an error. Tell students the sound, then back up two or more letters, and begin again.

Questions and Answers

or   ch   y

or   wh   th

al   or

y   or   ea   z

r   ck   ea   or

---

or

Activity 1

Letter-Sound Review

*(Hold up **or** letter-sound card.)*

Everybody, what sound?
/orr/

Again. What sound? /orr/

Individual Practice

(Give individual turns.)

(Hold up the book so all students can see the letters.)

Now it is time to review letter-sounds you have learned so far. When I touch under a letter-sound, tell me its sound. Keep saying its sound until I touch under the next letter-sound.

(Touch under the first or.) **What sound? /or/**

Individual Practice

(Provide individual practice with 3–4 letter-sounds per student.)

(Praise, mark the Mastery Sheet, and continue.)

241 Lesson 72

Letter-Sound Correspondence (Teacher's Edition B): Letter-Sound Dictation

Sounds with Multiple Spellings

Once students learn sounds that can be written in more than one way, they will be expected during Letter-Sound Dictation activities to write all the alternate ways they have learned. When dictating a sound that can be written more than one way, say, **You just wrote that sound one way; now write it another way.**

If students cannot retrieve all the ways they have learned for spelling a sound, use the letter-sound cards to remind them. Make sure alternate spellings that have not yet been taught are covered with sticky notes. Students should see only the spellings that have been previously introduced.

ACTIVITY AT A GLANCE

- Step 1: Begin letter-sound dictation as usual.
- Step 2: When you say a sound that can be written more than one way, remind your students to write the sound all the ways they can remember.

- Step 3: Correct all errors as they occur, checking for individual mastery.

IN THE REAL WORLD

Use the Letter-Sound Cards to remind students how a sound is written or of alternate spellings they may have forgotten to write.w

Questions and Answers

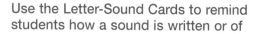

Lesson 72

Activity 2
Letter-Sound Dictation

(Have students turn to page 54 in Activity Book B.)

Look at the activity sheet. Now I will say some sounds, and you will write the letter or letters that stand for each sound. Write the letters one after another on the lined spaces. Make sure you leave a space between letter-sounds. Write as fast and as neatly as you can.

Note: When dictating the *l* and *le,* the *e* and *ea,* and the *ir, ur,* and *er,* say, "You just wrote that sound one way. Now write it another way."

(Hold continuous sounds for 2 seconds.)

Touch the first line with your pencil.
(Monitor.)

Listen. First sound. *(Pause.)* **/eee/**

Write the letter. Say the sounds as you write the letters.
(Monitor, scaffolding as necessary.)

Now write it another way.
(Monitor, scaffolding as necessary.)

> **Repeat the process with the following letter-sounds: /lll/ (written as l and -le), /y/, /or/, /rrr/, /z/, /th/ (as in them), /th/ (as in thin), /w/, /wh/, /err/ (spelled ir, ur, and er).**

242 Lesson 72

(If students make an error, have them correct it on the same line.)

(Monitor to make certain that students leave a space between the letter-sounds.)

Excellent job writing the letters from the sounds you hear! I will mark the Mastery Sheet so we can continue.

Name _____

Lesson 72

Activity 2

e ea l le y

or r z th th

w wh ir ur er

Activity 4

want   want want

eight   eight eight

Letter-Sound Correspondences (Teacher's Edition C)

Letter-Sound Correspondences activities in **Teacher's Edition C** continue as introduced and practiced in **Teacher's Editions A and B,** with Letter-Sound Introduction, Letter-Sound Review, and Letter-Sound Dictation.

Strand Three: Word Recognition and Spelling

In Word Recognition and Spelling activities, students begin looking at whole words and applying the skills they have learned in the Phonemic Awareness and Letter-Sound Correspondences strands to read and spell these words.

As students progress across lessons, words they read become increasingly complex. In the beginning, students read only two- and three-phoneme words consisting of closed syllable, VC (vowel-consonant), and CVC (consonant-vowel-consonant) patterns. To facilitate students' ability to sound out and easily read these initial words, the first letter in each word represents a continuous sound. From this initial stage, words gradually increase in complexity until students are easily reading two- and three-syllable words with all six syllable types represented.

Sounding out words may be difficult for students in the beginning. To facilitate the process, the words for Sounding Out activities will consist only of letter-sounds that have been previously taught. The skill is practiced with a few words each day. Students begin by sounding out words aloud, sound by sound. Students then move to reading words quickly, which is explained to students as "reading fast first." They also rapidly move into decoding.

The Sounding Out format changes quickly. First, students only sound out the word. Next, they sound out the word and then read it. Lessons quickly progress from having students read a list of words by sounding out and reading fast to reading the words in the list a second time fast first, without sounding out the word aloud. By the end of **Teacher's Edition C,** students are required to read fast first, without sounding out words.

SOUNDING OUT AT A GLANCE

Sounding Out

S a m

• • •

- Very difficult in the beginning
- Words to sound out contain only mastered sounds
- Practiced a little every day
- Moves quickly to Reading Fast First and then to Chunking

Sound It Out

Changes quickly

1. Sounding out the word
2. Sounding out the word, and then reading the word
3. Sounding out the word, and then reading the word again fast
4. Reading the word fast first

Sound Out in the Beginning

Format:

1. Hold up the **Teacher's Edition** so students can see the list.
2. Tell students to sound out the first word.
3. Touch under each sound while students say each sound in the word.
4. Touch under continuous sounds for two seconds, but move quickly off stop sounds.

Sounding-Out Format

"When I touch under the letter-sound, say its sound. Keep saying its sound until I touch under the next letter-sound."

S a m
→
• • •

Word Recognition and Spelling (Teacher's Edition A)

The Word Recognition and Spelling activities presented in **Teacher's Edition A** come from three categories of word recognition and spelling skills: Sounding Out, Tricky Words, and Stretch and Spell, which are discussed more fully in the order in which they are introduced in the program.

FORMATS

- Sounding Out
  - Sounding Out in the Beginning Lessons
  - Sounding Out and Reading Fast
  - Sounding Out and Reading Fast: Read It Again
  - What Word Now?
  - Forming Plurals
  - Reading Fast First
- Tricky Words, New and Review
- Stretch and Spell

Word Recognition and Spelling (Teacher's Edition A): Sounding Out

Sounding Out in the Beginning

All Sounding Out activities are presented initially using the **Teacher's Edition.** To present these activities, hold the **Teacher's Edition** at shoulder level so all students can see the word list. Tell students to sound out the first word. Guide students by touching under each letter-sound while they say each sound in the word.

When students are sounding out words, touch under continuous sounds for two or three seconds, but move off stop sounds quickly. A word being sounded out should sound like a word being stretched. There should be no pauses between sounds. In the early lessons, directional arrows and dots appear underneath the words as visual cues. These arrows and dots fade quickly. Dots reappear occasionally under a new letter-sound correspondence represented by a letter combination or when letters are doubled so that students know to read the letter combination as one sound.

ACTIVITY AT A GLANCE

- Step 1: Hold up the **Teacher's Edition** with the word list.
- Step 2: Tell students to sound out the first word.
- Step 3: Touch under each letter-sound while the students say the sounds in the word.

- Step 4: Touch under continuous sounds for two seconds, but move quickly off stop sounds.
- Step 5: Repeat the procedure with the remaining words.
- Step 6: End with individual mastery check by having students sound out one or two words each.

IN THE REAL WORLD

Students tend to rush their sounds when they first learn to sound out words. It is very important for you to model holding continuous sounds for two to three seconds. It is equally important to make sure your students are holding the sound for as long as you touch under the letter-sound. You may need to stop students and remind them that they need to stay together and that they need to say the sound as long as you touch under the letter-sound. Then start again. Holding continuous sounds makes sounding out easier for students. If you teach students to do this correctly in the beginning, they will be better able to handle reading word lists and connected text later in the intervention. Move off stop sounds quickly.

Questions and Answers

Lesson 5

Activity 7
Sounding Out

Now we are going to sound out words by putting together the sounds for all the letters in the word. My turn to sound out a word. Watch and listen. /Aaa/mmm/. (Touch under each letter as you say its sound. Hold each continuous sound for 2 seconds.)

When I touch under a letter, I say its sound. I keep saying its sound until I touch under the next letter. My turn again.
/Aaa/mmm/. (Again, touch under each letter as you say its sound.)

Now sound out this word with me. When I touch under the letter, say its sound. Keep saying its sound until I touch under the next letter.
Sound it out.
(Teacher and students:) /aaa/mmm/

Again, sound it out.
(Teacher and students:) /aaa/mmm/

Now by yourselves. Sound it out.
/aaa/mmm/

(Model-lead-test until all students can sound out am. Be sure students are answering in unison.)

Individual Practice
(Repeat with each student individually.)

Next word. My turn again.
/Aaa/t/. (Again, touch under each letter as you say its sound.)

Now sound out this word with me.
Sound it out.
(Teacher and students:) /aaa/t/

Again, sound it out.
(Teacher and students:) /aaa/t/

Now by yourselves. Sound it out. /aaa/t/

(Model-lead-test until all students can sound out at. Be sure students are answering in unison.)

Individual Practice
(Repeat with each student individually.)
Good sounding out. You have earned another check mark.

Sounding Out and Reading Fast

Sounding Out and Reading Fast is an activity that begins early in **Teacher's Edition A** and continues throughout **Teacher's Edition B.** To teach this format, hold the **Teacher's Edition** at shoulder level, and tell students to sound out the word. Students say each sound as you touch under the letter or letter combination.

As always, you touch under continuous sounds for approximately two seconds but move off stop sounds quickly. Students then read the word. Repeat this procedure with the remaining words. End with individual practice of one to two words per student to assess for individual mastery.

ACTIVITY AT A GLANCE

- Step 1: Hold up the **Teacher's Edition** with the word list.
- Step 2: Tell students to sound out the word.
- Step 3: Touch under each sound while the students say each sound in the word.
- Step 4: Touch under continuous sounds for two seconds but move quickly off stop sounds.
- Step 5: Ask students to read the word fast.
- Step 6: Repeat the procedure with the remaining words.
- Step 7: End with individual mastery check by having students read one or two words each.

IN THE REAL WORLD

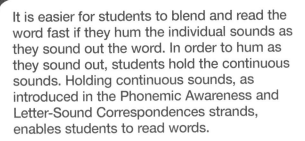

It is easier for students to blend and read the word fast if they hum the individual sounds as they sound out the word. In order to hum as they sound out, students hold the continuous sounds. Holding continuous sounds, as introduced in the Phonemic Awareness and Letter-Sound Correspondences strands, enables students to read words.

If your students are having trouble blending the word, it may be because you are moving too quickly from sound to sound and not holding continuous sounds long enough. Slow the sounding-out pace a little to see if this makes a difference for students. Once they can sound out the word and read it fast, smoothly, and without error, pick up the pace.

Questions and Answers

Activity 8
Sounding Out

(When you go through the list of words, distinguish between the letters m and n before sounding out each word.)

(Touch under the n in an.) **What is this letter's sound? /nnn/**

Sound it out. *(Slide your finger under each letter as students sound out.)* **/aaa/nnn/**
Read it fast. an

Repeat the process with the following words: ant, nat, *sat, **ram.

Note: *(When you come to the word sat, say:)*
The next 2 words have no dots. Sound them out the way you always do.
**(Touch under the m when you come to ram. Follow this procedure.)*
What is this letter's sound? /mmm/
Sound it out. /rrr/aaa/mmm/
Read it fast. ram

Individual Practice

(Provide individual practice.)

Good reading. What should I do now? Put a check mark on the lesson Mastery Sheet.

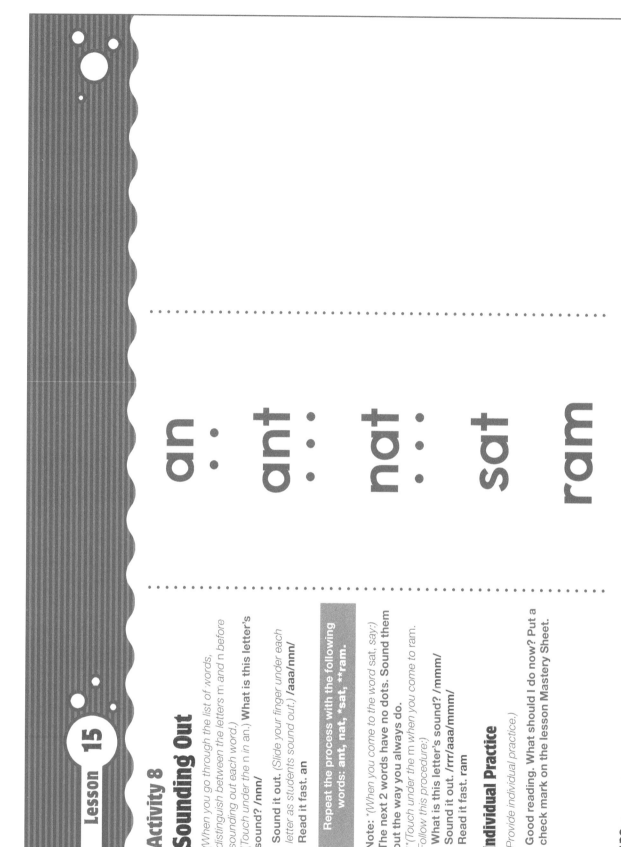

an

·

ant

· ·

nat

· ·

sat

ram

What Word Now?

The purpose of the **What Word Now?** activity is to teach students that the omission or addition of even one sound can effectively change the way a word is read as well as the word's meaning. In this activity, you write a word on the board. Students sound out the word and then read it fast. You then change the word by adding or removing only one letter.

ACTIVITY AT A GLANCE

- Step 1: Write a word on the board.
- Step 2: Have students sound out the word and read it fast.
- Step 3: Change the word by adding or removing one sound.
- Step 4: Students sound out and read the new word.
- Step 5: Repeat the procedure for the remaining words.
- Step 6: Provide individual practice with one or two words per student.

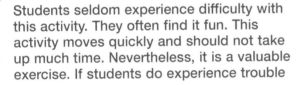

IN THE REAL WORLD

Students seldom experience difficulty with this activity. They often find it fun. This activity moves quickly and should not take up much time. Nevertheless, it is a valuable exercise. If students do experience trouble with the activity, this may indicate that they need additional practice Stretching and Blending and with Sounding Out and Reading Fast.

Questions and Answers

Lesson 18

Activity 6
What Word Now? Game

(Use the marker board for this game. Begin by writing the word Sam on the board.)

We are going to play a new game called What Word Now?

(Point to Sam, and say:) **Sound it out.**
/Sss/aaa/mmm/
Read it fast. Sam

(Erase S, and say:) **Now I will change it.** *(Point to am, and say:)* **Sound it out. /aaa/mmm/**

What word now? am
Yes! That is correct. Let's continue.

(Add r to the word am, and say:) **Now I'll change it. Sound it out. /rrr/aaa/mmm/**
What word now? ram

Repeat the process with the following words: ran, an, fan.

Individual Practice

(Provide individual practice with 1 word per student.)

(Praise students, put a check mark on the Mastery Sheet, and move to the next activity.)

151 Lesson 18

Forming Plurals

This skill is taught within the Sounding Out format. Students sound out the base word and read it fast. The plural ending -s is added to the word. Students then sound out the new word and read it fast.

ACTIVITY AT A GLANCE

- Step 1: Have the marker board ready with words from lesson written on it: *ant, mat, cat, rat.*
- Step 2: Students sound out the first word as you touch under the letters. **/aaa/nnn/t/**
- Step 3: Students read the base word. **ant**
- Step 4: Add -s to the base word to form the plural, as in the word *ants.*

- Step 5: Students sound out the new word as you touch under the letters. **/aaa/nnn/t/sss/**
- Step 6: Students read the new word. **ants**
- Step 7: Repeat the reading routine as described above with the remaining words.
- Step 8: End with individual mastery check by having students read both the singular and the plural form of a word.

IN THE REAL WORLD

If students have trouble pronouncing the plural, ask for the answer in sentence form. For example, **I have one cat. I have two cats.**

Then repeat the exercise until they can read the words in isolation.

Questions and Answers

Lesson 19

Activity 3
Plurals: Adding s

Inflectional Endings

(Cover the plural words on the next page and the illustrations to the right of the plural words with pieces of paper or sticky notes. Have a different piece of paper or note for each plural word and its illustration.)

(Point to the word ant.) **Sound it out.**
/aaa/nnn/t/

(Point to the picture of an ant.) **How many ants? one**

That is right. There is only one ant. Whenever we want to show more than one of something, we add an s or an es to the end of the word. Today we will talk about words that need only an s at the end to make a plural.

How do we show there is more than one of something? add s to the end of the word
(Uncover the word ants and the illustration of the two ants.)

(Point to the word ants.) **Sound it out.**
/aaa/nnn/t/sss/
Read it. ants

Again, how do you show more than one of something? Add s to the end of the word.

(Point to the word mat.) **Sound it out.**
/mmm/aaa/t/
Read it. mat

How do I show more than one mat? Add s to the end of the word.
(Uncover the word mats and the illustration of the two mats.) **What word now? mats**

> **Repeat the process with the following words: cat(s), rat(s).**

Individual Practice

(For each student, provide individual practice with 1 word and its plural.)

Good work, everyone. I will put a check mark on the Mastery Sheet, and we will continue with our next activity.

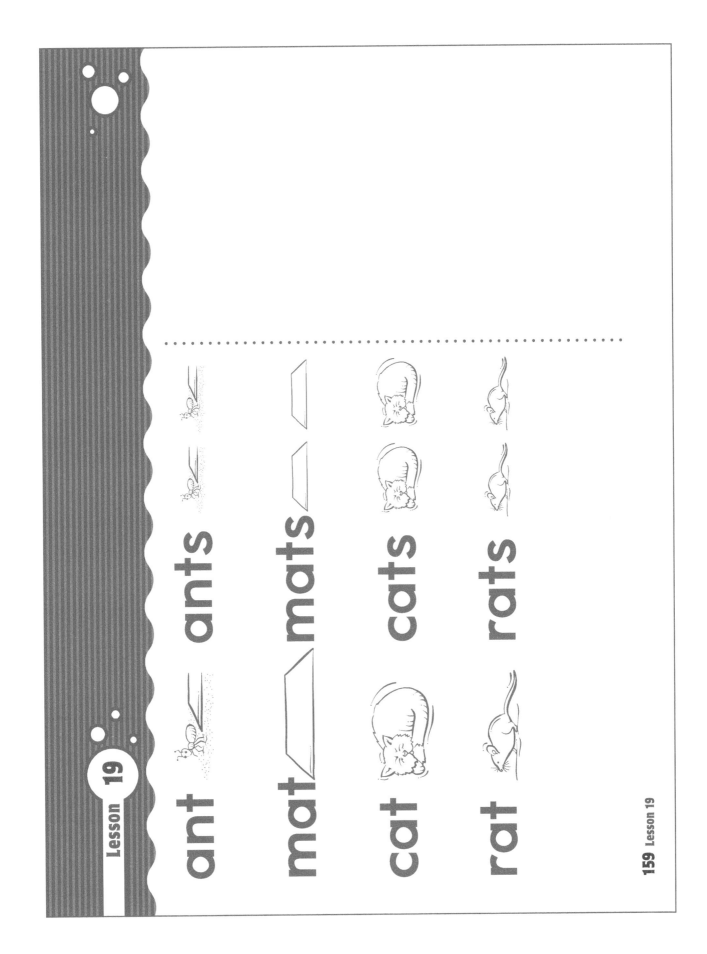

ant ants

mat mats

cat cats

rat rats

Sounding Out and Reading
Fast—Read It Again

Students sound out and read each word fast. Then they go back and read all the words fast the first time.

ACTIVITY AT A GLANCE

- Step 1: Students sound out each letter as you touch under it. Remember to touch under continuous sounds two or three seconds and to move off stop sounds quickly. Students should not pause between sounds.

- Step 2: Students read the word as you cue them by saying **Read it fast** and sliding your finger underneath the word.

- Step 3: Repeat the procedure with the remaining words.

- Step 4: Students go back and read all the words fast.

- Step 5: Build individual mastery by having students read one or two words each.

IN THE REAL WORLD

When students go back to read the words fast, they may find it difficult. If they make an error, have them sound out the word and read it fast. Then have them read the word fast again. Back up one or two words and have students read the words fast.

Questions and Answers

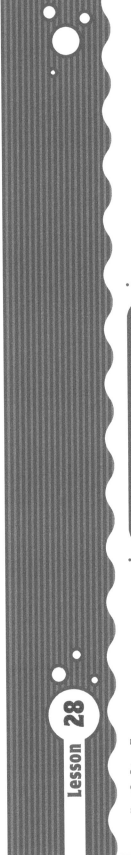

Lesson 28

Activity 4
Sounding Out
Teacher Led

Language and Literacy Support (ELD)

During this activity we will be sounding out some words, and I want to make sure you know all the words we will be reading.

The first word is *gift*. Who knows what a gift is? *(You may have to prompt further by saying:)* **Here is a hint. *My favorite gift was a blanket from my grandmother.*** *(Accept reasonable responses.)*

That's right. A gift is a present—something that one person gives to another person. Here is a picture of a gift. *(Hold up Pictures for Language and Literacy Support, page 30.)*

The next word is *miss*. Does anyone know what *miss* means? *(If students give another correct meaning, acknowledge it.)*

(You may have to prompt further by saying:) **What do I mean if I say *If I get sick, I have to miss a day of school?*** *(Accept reasonable responses.)*

Yes. *Miss* means "to not go somewhere you were planning to go."

Good job!

(Remember to hold continuous sounds 2 seconds, but quickly move off stop sounds. There should be no pauses between sounds when sounding out.)

Now you are going to sound out words. When I touch under a letter-sound, say the sound. Keep saying the sound until I touch under the next letter. Do not stop between sounds. Then read the word the fast way.

(Place your finger next to the word mats on the next page, and say:) **Sound it out.**
/mmm/aaa/t/sss/
Read it fast. mats

Repeat the process with the following words: miss, hand, pig, gift, fast.

mats

miss : • •

hand

pig

gift

fast

Individual Practice

(Give individual turns. Praise students and scaffold as necessary.)

Now you are going to read these words fast. When I place my finger under the word, I will cue you to answer by saying "Sound it out to yourselves" and then "Read it." Remember, I will give you time to think before you read it fast.

(Hold up your book, place your finger next to the word mats, and say:) **Sound it out to yourselves.**

(Pause.)

Read it. mats

Excellent. Let's continue.

Repeat the process with the remaining words: miss, hand, pig, gift, fast.

(Scaffold as necessary, going back to sound out a word if students have trouble.)

You are sounding out and reading words! Excellent!

(Praise students, put a check mark on the Mastery Sheet, and continue.)

234 Lesson 28

Reading Fast First

Once students have demonstrated competence in sounding out words and reading them fast, they learn that they don't have to sound out everything.

As a first step toward reading words automatically, without sounding out, students sound out the word in a whisper voice. Next you teach students to sound out words silently, in their heads, before reading the word aloud. Control how much time students are allowed to sound out in their heads by use of an auditory cue. Over time, allow less and less think time until students are reading words automatically.

ACTIVITY AT A GLANCE

- Step 1: Students sound out a word in their heads as you touch under each letter.
- Step 2: Give students one or two seconds of think time, and then cue them to read the word.
- Step 3: Repeat the procedure with the remaining words.
- Step 4: End with individual mastery check by having students read two or three words each.

IN THE REAL WORLD

If a student is having trouble reading a word, back up to an earlier format and scaffold the instruction by having students sound out the word in a whisper voice, one sound at a time, and then have them blend the sounds in the word. If they do this correctly, then have students read the word fast, back up two words, and begin again. If they still have trouble, use the Model-Lead-Test error-correction technique.

Questions and Answers

Lesson 32

cats

dog

fish.

cast

ship.

Activity 7
Reading Fast First

List

Here is a list of words you will read fast the first time. When I touch under the letters, sound out the word to yourselves. Then I will say, "Read it." I will give you time to think before you read it fast.

(Hold up the list, touch under the word cats, and say:) **Sound it out to yourselves.** *(Move your finger under each letter, holding under each letter for 2 seconds.)*

Read it. cats

Yes, cats. Next word. *(Pause.)* **Sound it out to yourselves.** *(Move your finger under each letter as before.)*

Read it. dog

Yes, *dog*. Next word.

> **Repeat the process with the following words: fish, cast, ship.**

(When students make an error, go back, sound out the word together in a whisper voice, and then say it fast.)

Individual Practice

(Give individual turns, and offer praise.)

Good job reading the list! I will put a check mark on the lesson Mastery Sheet, and we can continue.

Reading Fast First— Reduced Think Time

Think time provides the time necessary for students to sound out a word in their heads before they read the word. The amount of think time specified within the lesson is the maximum amount of time allowed between words. If students can sound out words in their heads and read the words faster than the specified think time, you can move the students faster. Pace students as fast as they can read. However, if many errors start to occur, allow more think time. The lowest-performing student determines the pace.

Mastery occurs if students can meet at least the specified maximum think time. The criterion must be met by the group.

Moving from Teacher Led to Student Led

Word Recognition and Spelling activities are first presented as teacher-led activities. After students have gained proficiency in reading words with the teacher leading the activity, they begin to read more independently. Student-led word recognition activities appear as word lists in **Activity Books.**

In student-led activities the students touch under each letter as they sound out the words while you control the pace by softly tapping. The goal for all activities is for the students to read words as accurately and independently as possible.

Word Recognition and Spelling (Teacher's Edition A): Tricky Words

Tricky Words

Tricky words are irregular high-frequency words. Certain words cannot be sounded out because not all of the letter-sound correspondences in a word have been introduced. In this case, the word is a tricky word only until all the sounds in the word have been introduced. Then the word is removed from the deck of tricky word cards. Some words contain letter-sound correspondences that are uncommon, so instead of teaching the alternative spelling, treat these words as tricky words. Other words are treated as tricky words because they contain *schwa* sounds as well as other irregular spelling patterns.

After each tricky word is introduced, students practice tracing, copying, and reading the word. Then each word is added to the deck of cards for review. Tricky words are reviewed in nearly every lesson. Automatic recognition of these words is necessary to promote fluent reading.

Tricky words are provided for you. Each card is numbered to help you organize.

I 1	the 2	The 3
is 4	Is 5	on 6

ACTIVITY AT A GLANCE

- Step 1: Review tricky words by holding them up one at a time and saying **What word?**
- Step 2: Introduce the new tricky word by holding up the card and saying **This word is _____ .**
- Step 3: Point to the new tricky word, and ask your students **What word?**
- Step 4: Model writing the new word. Say the word as you write the word.
- Step 5: Direct students to their activity sheets, and cue students to trace the word as they say the word.
- Step 6: After they have traced the word, cue students to copy the word as they say the word.
- Step 7: End with individual mastery check by letting each student read two or three words.

IN THE REAL WORLD

Having students say the word while they trace and copy the word further develops automatic word recognition of the new word.

Once enough tricky words have been introduced, the "Beat the Teacher Game" is introduced to increase motivation for your students during tricky word review. In this game the students score a point for every tricky word they read correctly, and you score a point for every word read incorrectly. The students take great pleasure in trying to beat the teacher. At the same time, students are developing automatic recognition of the tricky words.

If a tricky word is read incorrectly during review, tell students the word, have them read it together, put the card back in the deck, and give students another chance to read the word. Try to include any missed words in the individual mastery check.

Questions and Answers

Activity 7
Tricky Words

Review and New

(Use all the tricky word cards introduced to date.)

It's time to review the tricky words.

(Hold up a.)
What word is this? **a**
Yes, **a**.

> Repeat the process with the following tricky words: **A, have, is, I, the, on, The, Is, are.**

(Shuffle, and repeat.)

Individual Practice

(Provide individual practice with 2–3 words per student.)

Good job remembering our tricky words. *(Use Tricky Word Card— she.)* **Now we are going to learn a new tricky word.** *(Hold up she.)* **This word is** *she*. **What word is this?** *she*

(Direct students to the correct section of the activity sheet.)

You are going to trace the word *she*. Watch how I do it. As I trace *she*, I slowly say *she*. *(Model tracing she on a copy of the activity sheet or on the marker board.)* **What word did I trace?** *she*

Your turn. Trace the word *she*. **Say** *she* **as you trace the word.** *(Monitor.)* **What word did you trace?** *she*

Now I want you to copy the word *she* **on the lines below your tracing. Copy as neatly as you can. Slowly say** *she* **while you copy the word.**

> Repeat 2 times so students have written *she* a total of 3 times.

(Monitor.)

Good. We have finished another part of our lesson, and you know what that means. I will put a check mark on the Mastery Sheet.

Lesson 16

Activity 4

f	n	d	f
m	n	f	t

Activity 6

fan	Nan	man
ran	fat	Nat

Activity 7

she

she   she   she

Activity Book A

Word Recognition and Spelling (Teacher's Edition A): Stretch and Spell

The Stretch and Blend and Letter-Sound Dictation activities students have been practicing are preparing them for spelling words. As noted with Letter-Sound Dictation, it is easier for students to look at a letter and say the sound it represents than it is for them to hear a sound and then write the letter that represents that sound.

In Stretch and Spell activities, students spell words by stretching the word and listening for each individual sound they hear in the word. As the students listen for the individual sounds, they write each sound in the order they hear it.

The progression of Stretch and Spell mirrors the progression of Sounding Out. At first the students are stretching the words aloud while they write them. Eventually students stretch a spelling word in their heads before they spell it.

Stretch and Spell

In this format students stretch words and then spell them. Say a word, and have students stretch the word. Then have students write each sound in the correct order. On your cue, students read the word aloud.

If a student misspells a word, ask the student to stretch the word while looking at what he or she wrote. If the student has trouble stretching a word, you may need to model stretching the word.

ACTIVITY AT A GLANCE

- Step 1: Say the word.
- Step 2: Students stretch the word.
- Step 3: Students write each sound in the correct order.
- Step 4: Students read the word they spelled.
- Step 5: Repeat the procedure with the remaining words.

IN THE REAL WORLD

Use letter-sound cards to prompt students when necessary.

Questions and Answers

Activity 4
Stretch and Spell

(Have students open Activity Book A to page 18.)

Now I'll say a word, and you will spell it. First I'll say the word fast. Then you will stretch it. Listen for each sound as you stretch it. Then write the letter for each sound in the order you heard it. Write it fast. Write it neatly. No erasing.

Fists up.
Stretch *mat.* **mmm/aaa/t/**
(Hold up one finger for each sound.)

What word did you stretch? **mat**
Good job stretching. Now you will write the letters for the sounds you heard.

Get your pencils ready. *(Pause.)*
Spell *mat.*

Read the word you spelled. **mat**

(Scaffold as necessary.)

Great job hearing the sounds and spelling the word!

Listen to the next word. Fists up.
Stretch *rat.* **/rrr/aaa/t/**
(Hold up one finger for each sound.)
Write the letter for each sound in the order you heard it.

(Watch to see if each student writes the letters in the correct order. Repeat the word in stretched form as necessary.)
Read the word you spelled. **rat**

> Repeat the process with the following words: **Nat, sad, mad.**

(Scaffold as necessary.)

Good job listening and writing. We have finished this activity, and I am going to put a check mark on the Mastery Sheet.

Lesson 14

Activity 4

mat   rat

Nat

sad   mad

Activity 6

have   have

Activity 8

I am Sam.
• •   • •   • •

I am a rat.
• •   • •   • • •

I have a ram.
• •   • •   • •

Activity Book A

Word Recognition and Spelling (Teacher's Edition B)

The activities covered in the Word Recognition and Spelling Strand in **Teacher's Edition B** come from the same three categories of word recognition and spelling skills as in **Teacher's Edition A:** Sounding Out, Tricky Words, and Stretch and Spell. Activities encompass increasingly challenging word types, including multisyllabic words, inflectional word endings, tricky word analysis, and variant spellings.

Flexible Decoding

A unique feature of **SRA Early Interventions in Reading** is that students are taught to combine sounding out skills and context to decode irregular words. When you teach students to be flexible decoders, you prepare them to decode virtually any unknown word, even if the word does not sound out quite right. Usually the nondecodable sounds are close enough that students can figure out the word.

Students are taught that they should try multiple ways to read a word when a spelling has more than one sound (for example, *bead, bread*). Students also learn to deal with sounds that do not sound out quite right, like the *schwa* sound in an unstressed syllable *(abandon).* Words that require flexible decoding usually appear in the **Teacher's Edition** with an asterisk (*) and a note to the teacher to signal you to tell students they will need to flex a sound in a word.

FORMATS

- Sounding Out
  Early Multisyllabic Chunking
  Multisyllabic Chunking with Flexible Decoding
  Inflectional Endings
- Tricky Words—Analysis
- Stretch and Spell—Multiple Spellings

Word Recognition and Spelling (Teacher's Edition B): Sounding Out

Early Multisyllabic Chunking

Once students demonstrate proficiency reading monosyllabic CVC words, they begin to read two-syllable words. Reading multisyllabic words is taught using the multisyllabic chunking format. Multisyllabic words appear in the **Teacher's Edition** with chunks of sounds underlined. The students learn to sound out and read each part, read each part fast, and then read the whole word.

ACTIVITY AT A GLANCE

- Step 1: Students sound out and read each underlined part. **/rrr/aaa/b/ rabb /iii/t/ it**
- Step 2: Students read each part fast. **rabb it**
- Step 3: Students read the whole word. **rabbit**

- Step 4: Students read the word again the fast way. **rabbit**
- Step 5: End with individual mastery check by having students sound out and read one or two words each.

IN THE REAL WORLD

When students understand that a long word can be broken down into manageable chunks that can be sounded out, they are more comfortable reading multisyllabic words.

Sometimes students experience difficulty when reading the parts together. They tend to rush reading the parts and stumble over the word. Control their reading pace by telling students to read the part when you touch under the part, and then to read the next part only when you touch under it. Pick up the pace as the students get more comfortable with reading the parts.

Students sometimes have trouble pronouncing multisyllabic words because they are misplacing the accent or because a chunk may have a sound that does not sound out in a familiar way, such as a *schwa* sound. You may need to assist your students in tweaking the pronunciation until the word makes sense. For example, the second chunk in the word *panda* is pronounced /d/uuu/, not /d/aaa/ or /d/āāā/.

Questions and Answers

Activity 4
Sounding Out
Chunking—Teacher Led

Language and Literacy Support (ELD)

During this activity we will be sounding out some words, and I want to make sure you know all the words.

The first word is *habit*. Who knows what a habit is? *(You may have to prompt further by saying:)* **Here's a hint. I have a bad habit of biting my fingernails.** *(Accept reasonable responses.)*

That's right. A habit is something you do without thinking because you do it so often.

The next word is *cabin*. Does anyone know what a cabin is? *(You may have to prompt further by saying:)* **What do I mean if I say** *On the camping trip, we stayed in a log cabin?* *(Accept reasonable responses.)*

Yes. A cabin is a small one-story building. Here is a picture of a cabin. *(Hold up Pictures for Language and Literacy Support, page 43.)*

Good job!

(Remember to hold continuous sounds 2 seconds, but quickly move off stop sounds. Do not pause between sounds when sounding out.)

Today we will sound out big words. When we sound out big words, we sound them out in parts. First we sound out each underlined part, and then we read it fast. Next we read the underlined parts together. Then we read the entire word fast.

Listen. My turn. *(Touch under each sound in rabb.)* **/rrr/aaa/b/**
Now I will say the first part fast. *(Slide your finger under the rabb part.)* **rab**

Now I will sound out the second part. *(Touch under each sound in it.)* **/iii/t/**
Now I will say the second part fast. *(Slide your finger under the it part.)* **it**

Next I will say the parts together. *(Touch under each part as you say it.)* **rab** *(Pause.)* **it Here's the whole word. Rabbit.**

(Hold up the word list on the next page. Place your finger under the word rabbit, and say:) **Your turn.**

Sound out the first part. *(Touch under each sound in rabb.)* **/rrr/aaa/b/**
(Slide your finger under the rabb part, and say:) **Say this part fast. rab**

(Touch under each sound in it.) **Sound it out. /iii/t/**

(Slide your finger under the it part, and say:) **Say this part fast. it**

Now say the parts together. *(Touch under each part as students say the part.)* **rab** *(Pause.)* **it**
Read the whole word. rabbit

Note: Remind students that the /b/ sound is said only once. If students say "rab—bit," tell them, "That is not quite right. We don't say *rab—bit*; we say *rab—it*."

Repeat the process with the following words: habits, cabin.

Individual Practice
(Give individual turns.)

Lesson 44

Now we will read these words fast the first time. When I place my finger next to the word, I will cue by saying "Sound it out to yourselves," and then "Read it." Remember, I will give you time to think before you read it fast.

(Hold up the word list. Touch under the word rabbit, and say:) **Sound it out to yourselves.** *(Slowly slide your finger under each letter.)* **Read it.** *(Slash your finger quickly under the word from left to right.)* **rabbit**

Very good. Let's continue.

Repeat the process with the following words: habits, cabin.

(Scaffold as necessary, going back to sound out a word if students missed it.)

Individual Practice

(Give individual turns.)

You are sounding out and reading words! Excellent!

(Praise students, mark off this activity on the Mastery Sheet, and continue.)

rabbit

habits

cabin

30 Lesson 44

Multisyllabic Chunking with Flexible Decoding

Multisyllabic chunking progresses quickly so that the sounding-out step is removed. Students are prompted to sound out each part silently before reading the part fast. Later, students read the word parts fast without sounding out, and then they read the whole word.

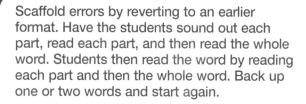

ACTIVITY AT A GLANCE

- Step 1: Students say the first part. **an**
- Step 2: Students say the second part. **i**
- Step 3: Students say the next part (for words with more than two parts): **mals**
- Step 4: Students say all the parts. **an i mals**
- Step 5: Students read the whole word smoothly. **animals**
- Step 6: End with independent practice of one or two words per student.

IN THE REAL WORLD

Scaffold errors by reverting to an earlier format. Have the students sound out each part, read each part, and then read the whole word. Students then read the word by reading each part and then the whole word. Back up one or two words and start again.

When students are trying to read words with three chunks, it can be awkward for them. You may need to help them by discussing how one chunk can be stressed or accented more than the others. It may be that they are trying to say the chunks too quickly. Slow the pace, and teach students that they do not have to rush the chunks when they are reading the whole word.

Questions and Answers

Lesson 79

Activity 6
Sounding Out

Chunking—Teacher Led

(Hold up the word list on the next page, and say:) **These are words in the story that we will read later. When you read big words, say each part. Then read the whole word fast.**

(Place your finger under the word Henetta. Slide your finger under the Hen part, and say:) **Say this part. Hen**

(Slide your finger under the ett part, and say:) **Say this part. ett**

(Slide your finger under the a part, and say:) **Now say this part. a**

Note: Explain the schwa sound in *Henetta* for students. The schwa a sounds like /uh/.

Now say the parts together. *(Touch under each part as students say it.)* **Hen** *(pause)* **ett** *(pause)* **a**

Read the whole word. Henetta

> **Repeat the process with the following words: *abandon, *water, bucket, animals, monster.**

Note: **Before each word with an asterisk, say,* "This word almost sounds out right."

The a in Henetta, the a in water, and the first a and the o in abandon do not sound out correctly.

Individual Practice

(Give individual turns.)

Now you will read these words fast.

(Hold up the word list. Place your finger under the word Henetta, and say:) **First word.**

(Pause 3 seconds.)

Read it. *(Slash your finger from left to right underneath the word.)* **Henetta**

> **Repeat the process with the following words: abandon, water, bucket, animals, monster.**

(Scaffold as necessary, going back to sound out a word if students miss it.)

Individual Practice

(Provide individual practice with reading the list fast.)

(Praise students, mark the Mastery Sheet, and continue.)

296 Lesson 79

Henetta

abandon

water

bucket

animals

monster

Inflectional Endings

Several inflectional endings are introduced to students in this curriculum. Endings are added to show plurality *(cat/cats)*, past tense *(dance/danced)*, and state of being *(talk/talking)*. Students learn the ending and then practice reading words with the ending. First students read the base word, and then they read the new word. When the last letter is doubled before adding the ending, briefly note this change for your students.

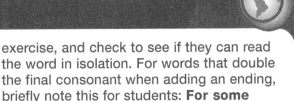

ACTIVITY AT A GLANCE

- Step 1: Have the marker board ready with the base words from the lesson written in a column.
- Step 2: Students read the word list with no endings.
- Step 3: Underline each base word and add the ending. Double the last letter when appropriate.
- Step 4: After adding the ending, say **Read the underlined part** (base word). **Read the whole word** (base word + ending).
- Step 5: Students read the base word, and then they read the whole word. **pull—pulled**
- Step 6: Repeat the reading routine for the remaining words.
- Step 7: End with individual mastery check by having each student read one or two words with the endings.

IN THE REAL WORLD

Students may experience difficulty pronouncing the *-ed* ending at the end of a word once they have learned all three sounds it stands for (*/t/, /d/, /ed/*). Using the word in a sentence can help build familiarity with the pronunciation. Once the students are comfortable with the word, return to the exercise, and check to see if they can read the word in isolation. For words that double the final consonant when adding an ending, briefly note this for students: **For some words, we have to double the last letter before adding the ending.**

Questions and Answers ·

Lesson 68

Activity 5
Adding Endings
_ed and _ing

(Write the following words in a column on the marker board: pull, help, pass, pack, hop, step.) **Now it is time to read these words fast the first time. When I tap under a word, read it.**

(Tap under pull, and say:) **This word almost sounds out right.**
Read it. *(Pause 2 seconds, and then tap.)* **pull**

(Scaffold as necessary.)

(Write the _ed ending on the board, and say:) **Now I will add this ending to these words.**

(Underline the base, and add _ed to each word. Double the last letter when necessary.)

(Tap under pulled, and say:) **Read the underlined part.** *(Pause 2 seconds, and then tap.)* **pull**
Read the whole word. *(Pause 2 seconds, and then tap.)* **pulled**

> Repeat the process with the following words: **helped, passed, packed, hopped, stepped.**

(Scaffold as necessary.)

Individual Practice

(Give individual turns.)

(Erase the _ed endings from the base words. Write the _ing ending on the board, and say:) **Now I will add this ending to these words.**

(Add _ing to each word. Double the last letter when necessary.)

(Tap under pulling, and say:) **Read the underlined part.** *(Pause 2 seconds, and then tap.)* **pull**
Read the whole word. *(Pause 2 seconds, and then tap.)* **pulling**

> Repeat the process with the following words: **helping, passing, packing, hopping, stepping.**

(Scaffold as necessary.)

Individual Practice

(Give individual turns.)

You did a great job adding endings to words! I will mark the Mastery Sheet, and we will continue with the next activity.

Word Recognition and Spelling (Teacher's Edition B): Tricky Words

Analysis of Tricky Words

A unique feature of the curriculum is that students are taught to be flexible decoders. They are taught that if they do not know a word, they should be able to sound it out. They also learn that not all words sound out quite right. As part of learning flexible decoding, students are asked to analyze tricky words to determine the parts that do not sound out in a familiar way.

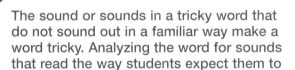

ACTIVITY AT A GLANCE

- Step 1: Hold up the new tricky word card, and read the word.
- Step 2: Sound out the tricky word, reading it the way it sounds out.
- Step 3: Point out the sounds in the word that sound out correctly.
- Step 4: Have students read the new tricky word the correct way.

- Step 5: Repeat the procedure with any other new tricky words in the lesson.
- Step 6: Add new tricky word cards to the review deck, and review all the tricky words introduced so far.
- Step 7: End with individual mastery check by having each student read two or three words. Make sure each student has an opportunity to read each new word.

IN THE REAL WORLD

The sound or sounds in a tricky word that do not sound out in a familiar way make a word tricky. Analyzing the word for sounds that read the way students expect them to and identifying the sounds that do not help students build familiarity with the tricky word. Repetitive reading of tricky words leads to automatic recognition.

Questions and Answers

Activity 4
Tricky Words
New and Review

(Have students turn to page 54 in Activity Book B. Have available all the tricky word cards introduced to date as well as Tricky Word Cards—want and eight.)

Today you are going to learn two new tricky words.

(Hold up want, *and say:)* **This word is** *want.*
What word? *want*

Let's see if we can sound out that word. Sound it out. *(Point to each letter as students sound out* want.*) /www/aaa/nnn/t/*

Yes. That is how we sound out the word. But we say *want,* **not** */www/aaa/nnn/t/.* **The** *w, n,* **and** *t* **say their sounds correctly and can help you figure out the word by yourself.**

One more time.
What word? *want*

(Hold up eight, *and say:)* **This word is** *eight.*
What word? *eight*

Sound out *eight.* */eee/iii/g/h/t/*
This word can't be sounded out! The *t* **is the only letter that says its sound the usual way.**

One more time.
What word? *eight*

Individual Practice

(Provide each student the chance to read both words.)

(Direct students to the correct section of the activity sheet.)

Now you will write these words. Look at the activity sheet. Finish writing the word *want* **on the first line. The letter** *a* **has been printed for you, because it does not sound out in the usual way. Write the letters that do say their sounds right.**
Listen. *Want.*
Write the missing letters.

(Monitor, and correct if necessary.)

Now write the whole word. Slowly say the word *want* **as you write** *want.*

(Monitor, and correct if necessary.)

Write the word *want* **one more time on the same line. Make sure to leave a space between words.**

Repeat the process with the word eight.

(Add want *and* eight *to the deck of tricky words.)*

Please keep your activity books open, because we will use them later.

Now it is time to review the tricky words.

(Hold up I.*)* **Read it.** I

Repeat the process with all the tricky words.

(Shuffle the deck, and repeat unison responding.)

(If students make an error, return the card to the deck, and repeat.)

Individual Practice

(Provide individual practice with 3–4 tricky words per student. Make sure each student has the chance to read want *and* eight.*)*

Good job reading the tricky words. You have finished another activity. I will put a check mark on the Mastery Sheet so we can continue.

Lesson 72

Activity 2

e   ea   l   le   y

or   r   z   th   th

w   wh   ir   ur   er

Activity 4

want   want want

eight   eight eight

Activity Book B

Word Recognition and Spelling (Teacher's Edition B): Stretch and Spell

Words with Sounds that Have Multiple Spellings

Many words have sounds that can be represented multiple ways. At this point in the program, students are asked to spell words with sounds that can be represented more than one way. At first you will tell the students which way the sounds are spelled, using the letter-sound cards to illustrate. For example, before students spell the word *bird,* point under *ir* on the /er/ card and say, **/er/ is spelled this way.**

Later, students will spell words without being prompted. However, you will have the letter-sound cards for those sounds ready to use for correcting errors. Other words will represent spelling rules that have been introduced, such as spelling words with the silent e on the end. You may need to remind students of any rules that apply to the words they are spelling.

ACTIVITY AT A GLANCE

- Step 1: Use the letter-sound cards to prompt students to use the correct spelling of the sound in a specific word.
- Step 2: At first, you will review the correct way to spell the sound before students spell a word.
- Step 3: Later, students try to spell the word alone; prompt only if necessary.
- Step 4: Say the word.

- Step 5: Students stretch the word in their heads.
- Step 6: Students write each sound in the correct order they hear it.
- Step 7: Students read aloud the word they spelled.
- Step 8: Repeat the procedure with the remaining words, checking for individual mastery.

IN THE REAL WORLD

Have ready letter-sound cards, with previously introduced alternate spellings uncovered. If students write the correct sound but do not choose the correct spelling for that sound, let them know that what they wrote does say the right sound, but then point to the correct spelling, and say, This is how we spell this sound in this word.

Questions and Answers

Staff Development Guide, Level 1

Lesson 66

Activity 3
Stretch and Spell

(Have available the er and wh letter-sound cards. Direct students to the correct section of the activity sheet.)

Now you will stretch and spell some words. First I will say the word fast. Then you will stretch the word to yourselves.

I will give you time to think while you stretch the word to yourselves. Then write the letters for the sounds in the correct order.

Listen. *(Pause.)* **Pond.** *(Pause.)* Stretch *pond* in your head. *(Pause.)* Write each sound in the correct order.

(Monitor to see if each student writes the letters in the correct order.)

Read the word you spelled. **pond**

(If students make an error, go back, and sound out the word together.)

Repeat the process with the following words: bats, sled, dish, *bird, *when.

Note: *If necessary, hold up the appropriate letter-sound card when students are writing bird and when.

(Scaffold as necessary.)

Language and Literacy Support

I want to check to see if you know what the words we just wrote mean.

The first word is *bats*. Who knows what *bats* are? *(If students give another correct meaning, acknowledge it, but focus on the contextual meaning in Story-Time Reader 29, In the Pond, which students will read later in this lesson.)*

(You may have to prompt further by saying:) Here's a hint. *We saw some bats flying through the trees at the zoo. (Accept reasonable responses.)*

That's right. Bats are flying animals that find food at night. They are not birds, but their front feet are stretched out to form wings. Bats eat fruit, small animals, and insects. They can even hang upside-down! This is a picture of some bats. *(Hold up Pictures for Language and Literacy Support, page 67.)*

The next word is *sled*. Who knows what a *sled* is? *(You may have to prompt further by saying:)* Here's a hint. *The day after the big snowstorm, the children went to Harris Hill to sled. (Accept reasonable responses.)*

Sled is an action, or verb, that means to slide down a snow-covered hill.

A sled is also a thing, or noun—the object on which you slide down the hill. Here is a picture of a boy on a sled. *(Hold up Pictures for Language and Literacy Support, page 68.)*

The last word is *dish*. Who knows what a dish is? *(You may have to prompt further by saying:)* What do I mean if I say *My father handed me another dirty dish to wash? (Accept reasonable responses.)*

That's right. *Dish* is another word for a plate or bowl. This is a picture of a dish. *(Hold up Pictures for Language and Literacy Support, page 69.)*

Good listening and writing!

(Mark off this activity on the Mastery Sheet, and continue.)

---

203 Lesson 66

Name _____

Lesson 66

Activity 2

| th | th | x | ar | u |
| wh | w | e | i | o |

Activity 3

pond bats sled

dish bird when

Activity 4

pigs pond cats hopped neck help

Activity 5

four four four four

five five five five

too too too too

Activity Book B

41

Staff Development Guide, Level 1

Word Recognition and Spelling (Teacher's Edition C)

The activities covered in the Word Recognition and Spelling Strand in **Teacher's Edition C** come from the same three categories of word recognition and spelling skills as in **Teacher's Editions A and B:** Sounding Out, Tricky Words, and Stretch and Spell.

There are no format changes for Tricky Words and Stretch and Spell activities in **Teacher's Edition C.** Both skills continue to reflect increasingly complex word types. In Sounding Out activities, students continue sounding out words in their heads when chunking multisyllabic words as well as flexing sounds that do not sound out quite right. Students learn the silent-e rule, to read words or syllables that end with a vowel, and to attend to complex elements within a word before reading the word.

FORMATS

- Sounding Out
  CVC versus VCe (silent *e*)
  Introducing CV Pattern
  Part-Whole

Word Recognition and Spelling (Teacher's Edition C): Sounding Out

CVC versus VCe (Silent e)

One of the most difficult patterns to teach students is the VCe pattern. Students have to learn to use the final e as a tool for determining the correct pronunciation of the preceding vowel and that the final e is not actually pronounced.

In *SRA Early Interventions in Reading* students are taught the "silent-e rule." This rule is **When there is an e on the end of a word, the vowel says its name.** This pattern is also taught as a combination letter-sound. To teach this rule, point to the e in a VCe word and say, **When there is an e,** (point under the preceding vowel) **the vowel says its name.**

After learning the rule, students apply the rule. Students read VCe words, working through a series of steps. For each word, point under the e, and ask, **Is there an e?** Next, point under the vowel and ask, **What will the vowel say?** Last, ask students to read the word.

To facilitate rapid recognition of the VCe pattern, students are also taught to recognize the long-vowel patterns *a_e, e_e, i_e, o_e,* and *u_e* automatically as part of the Letter-Sound Correspondences Strand.

Once students have learned the "silent-*e*" rule and are reading VCe words easily, they will be asked to discriminate between CVC *(hop)* and VCe *(hope)* words. Prior to beginning this format, students have practiced listening for long and short vowels in the Phonemic Awareness Strand.

ACTIVITY AT A GLANCE

- Step 1: Hold up the list of words with the vowel in the middle of each word underlined.

- Step 2: Remind students of the silent-*e* rule.

- Step 3: Point to the list. Point to the first word, and ask, **Is there an e at the end?**

- Step 4: Point to the vowel in the word. Ask, **What will the vowel say?**

- Step 5: Ask students to read the word.

- Step 6: Repeat the procedure with the remaining words. Correct all errors as they occur.

- Step 7: End with individual mastery check by having students read one or two words.

IN THE REAL WORLD

This activity promotes the awareness that there may be more than one way to read a letter. Students may say the name of the letter, but when they read the word they may use the letter's sound (*mad* instead of *made*). Tell students they used the letter's sound instead of the letter's name. Touch under the vowel in the word, and say, ***What's this letter's name?*** Then touch under each letter in the word, and have students sound it out before reading it fast again.

Questions and Answers

nice nick

cat Kate

Nat Nate

Activity 5
Vowel Sounds

CVC and VCe

(Have the A—vowel and I—vowel letter-sound cards ready.)

(Point to the e in the a_e and i_e on the letter-sound cards.)

What is the rule about silent e? When there is an e at the end of a word, the letter says its name.

Very good. When there is an e at the end of a word, these letters *(point to a and i on the letter-sound cards)* **say their names.**

Let's practice some words that use the silent-e rule.

(Hold up the list so all students can see the words. Touch under the word nice.) **Is there an e? Yes.**

(Now point to the i in the word nice.) **Think.** *(Pause 3 seconds.)*

What word? nice

Yes, nice. Next word.

Repeat the process with the following words: nick, cat, Kate, Nat, Nate.

Note: If necessary, remind students about the ce rule for the word nice.

Individual Practice

(Provide individual practice.)

(Have students open Activity Book C to page 24. Direct students to the correct section of the activity sheet.)

Everyone, touch the first word on your activity sheet. *(Monitor.)*
Is there an e at the end of the word? Yes. Think. *(Pause 3 seconds.)*
What word? plate

Yes, plate. Next word.

Repeat the process with the following words: nut, chop, date, nine, shake, pinch, that, slice, ripe, spice, cake.

Individual Practice

(Provide individual practice.)

(Have students keep their activity books open for the next activity; put a check mark on the Mastery Sheet, and continue.)

Lesson 92

Activity 3

twins	spine
tree	nine
ten	slide
time	slim

Activity 5

pl_a_te   n_u_t   ch_o_p   d_a_te

n_i_ne   sh_a_ke   p_i_nch   th_a_t

sl_i_ce   r_i_pe   sp_i_ce   c_a_ke

CV Pattern (Open Syllable)

When students have learned the sounds for the vowels, they are taught how to determine if the vowel should be pronounced as a short sound or as a long sound. By this time in the program, students are proficient in reading closed-syllable words. Students already know how to pronounce the short-vowel sound in these words. All that is needed is a rule to help them recognize when a vowel is a long vowel.

Because the terms *long* and *short vowels* are not used, students are told that *a, e, i, o,* and *u* sometimes say their sound and sometimes say their name. They are then taught the rule that if words end with one of these letters, the letter usually says its name. Students are then provided multiple opportunities to apply the rule.

ACTIVITY AT A GLANCE

- Step 1: Explain the rule to students. **If a word or a syllable ends with a vowel, the vowel usually says its name.**
- Step 2: Review the rule with students. **If a word or a syllable ends with a vowel, what will the vowel say?**

- Step 3: Students answer **Its name.**
- Step 4: Students read words that end with vowels.
- Step 5: End with individual practice of one or two words per student.

IN THE REAL WORLD

Correct errors as soon as they occur with Model-Lead-Test.

Questions and Answers

Activity 7

Introducing the CV Pattern

(On the right side of the marker board, write the following items: _a, _e, _i. On the left side, write the following words, with the e underlined in each word: he, be, she, the, we, me. Have available Tricky Word Cards—the, The, she, he, me, be.)

Here is a new rule to follow. If a word or a part of a word *(syllable)* **ends with a vowel** *(point to the _a),* **the vowel usually says its name.**

If a word or a syllable ends with a vowel *(point to the _a),* **what will the vowel say? its name**

> **Repeat the process with the following vowels: _e, _i.**

Good. Let's try some words that follow the rule.

(Point to the _e.) **These words all end with e.**

(Point to he.) **What word? he**

> **Repeat the process with the following words: be, she, *the, we, me.**

Note: *Explain that the word the is pronounced /th/ /eee/ or /th/ /uh/.*

Now that we know this rule, I am going to remove the words the, The, she, he, me, and be from the deck.

(Hold up each tricky word card as you remove it from the deck. Ask students to read the word as you remove the card.)

Note: These are open-syllable words. An open syllable ends with a vowel, and the vowel says its name. An open syllable can be only 1 letter if that letter is a vowel. For example, the words *I* and *A* and the syllable *o* in *open* are open syllables. Some students may be familiar with this concept. If students ask if the words in this activity are open-syllable words, tell them yes.

Student Assessment

(After completing Lesson 92, please turn to Assessment 14 in the Placement and Assessment Guide. Administer the test to individual students.)

Part-Whole Format

Once students are reading words automatically, it is important to reinforce reading through the whole word. The Part-Whole format teaches students to attend to complex elements within words before reading the word.

In this format, a complex element, such as a diphthong or an *r*-controlled vowel, is underlined. Students first read the underlined part and then read the entire word.

ACTIVITY AT A GLANCE

- Step 1: Students read the underlined part.
- Step 2: Students read the word.
- Step 3: Repeat the procedure with the remaining words.
- Step 4: End with individual mastery check by having students read one or two words each.

IN THE REAL WORLD

Scaffold errors by having students sound out words and read them fast. Then back up one to two words, and begin again.

Questions and Answers . . . .

Activity 3

Reading Fast First

Lists

Language and Literacy Support ⓔⓛⓓ

During this activity we will be reading some words, and I want to make sure you understand them all.

The first word is *switch*. Does anyone know what switch means? (*If students give another correct meaning, acknowledge it, but focus on the contextual meaning in* **Story-Time Reader 37**, *Patch Gets the Ball, which students will read later in this lesson.*)

(*You may have to prompt further by saying:*) Here's a hint. I like your sticker, and you like mine. Why don't we switch? (*Accept reasonable responses.*)

That's right. Switch means to trade something with someone. Switch places with the person next to you. (*Indicate one student.*)

What did you do? switched places

Yes. You switched places with the person next to you.

The next word is *bushes*. Who knows what bushes are? (*You may have to prompt further by saying:*) Here's a hint. When we play hide-and-seek, I like to hide in the bushes in the yard. (*Accept reasonable responses.*)

Yes. Bushes are plants that grow outward. They look like short, fat trees. Many people plant bushes to make their yards look more beautiful. Here is a picture of some bushes. (*Hold up Patch Gets the Ball, page 5.*)

The next word is *splash*. Who knows what splash means? (*You may have to prompt further by saying:*) Here's a hint. When I jump in the pool, I splash water everywhere!

Yes. *Splash* means "to throw water or other liquid around." Here is a picture of someone making a big splash in the bathtub. (*Hold up page 7 of Story-Time Reader 36,* Seth's Bath, *which was introduced in Lesson 80.*)

Great job!

Note: Remember, saying the sounds for letter combinations in isolation is easier than decoding those sounds in words. Reading the underlined units first helps students read the whole word.

We are going to read some words. First say the sound of the underlined part. Then read the whole word.

My turn to do the first word. (*Point to tch in the word* Patch *on the next page.*)
First I will say the sound of the underlined part. (*Pause 2 seconds.*) /ch/
Now I will read the whole word. (*Pause 2 seconds.*) Patch.

Your turn. First word. (*Pause 2 seconds.*)
Say the sound. /ch/ (*Pause 2 seconds.*)
Read the word. Patch

Next word. (*Pause 2 seconds.*)
Say the sound. /er/ (*Pause 2 seconds.*)
Read the word. winter

Repeat the process with the following words: switch, splash, catch, parks, chunk, birds, *bushes, tossed.

Note: *Bushes is a flex word because it almost sounds out right.

Individual Practice

(*Provide individual practice.*)

Good job reading words fast. I will mark off this activity on the Mastery Sheet, and we can continue.

Patch

switch

catch

chunk

bushes

winter

splash

parks

birds

tossed

Strand Four: Fluency

The Fluency Strand is designed to build reading fluency. When a reader is fluent, she or he is able to decode text accurately and automatically. Two components of fluency are accuracy and speed. Accuracy is the fluent reading of unknown words and the immediate recognition of previously encountered words. Speed is the smoothness with which an individual reads connected text.

Fluency directly affects comprehension. Students who struggle to read tend to have weak comprehension skills. In the Fluency Strand, students are provided with plenty of opportunities to read text that is familiar, predictable, and decodable in order to develop fluency.

Fluency is measured as words per minute (wpm). Once students are reading all the words in a story "fast first," begin to monitor fluency by timing readings. (Timed readings begin in Lesson 33.) When monitoring begins, students are initially expected to be reading only about 20 wpm. The fluency goal increases about 2 wpm per week. At the same time the text becomes more difficult. By the end of the intervention materials, students attain normal fluency levels of 60 wpm on end-of-first-grade text.

When fluency monitoring begins, a fluency goal is provided for each story. If students meet these goals for the stories, they are well on their way to becoming fluent readers. Preview each story-reading activity before working with students so you know what to expect of them.

Fluency (Teacher's Editions A, B, C): Reading Connected Text

Reading progresses through several phases in the Fluency Strand. Students begin reading connected text by sounding out and reading fast one to five sentences from the **Teacher's Edition.** Then students begin to read short stories printed on their activity sheets. As soon as students are reading text on their own, the **Story-Time Readers** are introduced.

The first few **Story-Time Readers** are rebus stories. Rebus text consists of tricky words and pictures only, providing practice for the students in reading the tricky words they have learned thus far. Quickly, students transition to reading normal text that gradually becomes more complex over the course of the lessons, but they are never asked to read text for which they do not yet possess the necessary skills.

In **Teacher's Edition B, Challenge Stories** are introduced. These stories follow the same reading format as the **Story-Time Readers** and are introduced only when students have met the specified fluency criteria for the main reading selection. **Challenge Stories** allow for additional reading practice on text for which students have mastered the necessary decoding skills. Both **Story-Time Readers** and **Challenge Stories** are short, decodable stories that allow students to apply the skills and knowledge they have gained in the curriculum.

Fluency (Teacher's Edition A): Reading Simple Text

Simple Text—Teacher Led

The Fluency Strand starts with simple text presented using the **Teacher's Edition.** To teach this format, hold the **Teacher's Edition** so all students can see the text. Use your finger as a visual guide for students to follow in order to read in unison. For each decodable word, say **Sound it out,** moving your finger under each letter. Then ask, **What word?** For each tricky word, say **Read it** as you tap quickly under the word. After students have sounded out and read the sentence, say **Read it fast.** Students go back and read the sentence the fast way.

In the first few lessons, directional arrows and dots are underneath the words as another visual cue for students. The arrows and dots gradually fade. Dots reappear occasionally under a letter that is represented by a letter combination or when letters are doubled so students know to read them as one sound.

Reading simple text begins as a teacher-led, sounding-out, and reading-fast activity and progresses to student-led Reading Fast First by the end of **Teacher's Edition A.** When the activity is student-led, students read from their **Activity Books,** following along with their fingers. Maintain unison responses by softly tapping on the table once for each word. Think time per word is specified in the activity.

ACTIVITY AT A GLANCE

- Step 1: Hold up the story in **Teacher's Edition** so students can see the story.

- Step 2: For each decodable word say **Sound it out,** moving your finger under each letter. For each tricky word say **Read it,** and tap under the word.

- Step 3: After the students have sounded out the sentence, they read it the fast way. Say **Read it fast** as you slide your finger under each decodable word, and touch quickly under tricky words.

- Step 4: Repeat the procedure with the remaining sentences.

- Step 5: End with individual practice of one sentence per student. Do not tap during individual practice.

IN THE REAL WORLD

Take the time to train your students to read a word only on your tap. If they are not reading together, stop them, repeat your instruction to read only when you tap, and start again. Unison reading allows you to monitor all your students at the same time and gives optimal reading time to each student.

Students read sentences until they can read smoothly.

When students are sounding out a word, touch under each letter, holding continuous sounds and moving off stop sounds quickly.

Questions and Answers

If your students make an error as they read a sentence, have them sound out the word and read it fast. Then have them go back to the beginning of the sentence and begin again.

If students are making a lot of errors, slow the pace a bit. Once they are able to read the words smoothly, you can have them read the sentence faster.

Activity 9

Connected Text— Teacher Led

Fluency Development

Note: Follow this format: For each tricky word, tap under the word. For each word students can decode, slide your finger under each letter. Students sound out the word and then read it fast. Finally students read each sentence fast. If students hesitate, use the following cues: "Read it" for tricky words, "Sound it out" for decodable words, and "Read it fast" after they sound out the sentence.

We are going to read a story about two rats. When I tap under the tricky words, read them. For the words with the dots, I will slide my finger under the letters, and you will sound them out and then say the words. After you finish sounding out a sentence, read it the fast way.

Note: If students are capable of doing so, they may read the sentences fast the first time. However, students should read and reread the sentences until they can read smoothly and without any mistakes.

Read the first sentence by yourselves today. I /aaa/mmm/ am /Nnn/aaa/t/ Nat. I am Nat.
Great reading. Continue reading.

Repeat the process with remaining sentences.

Look at the last sentence. It has no dots. Read it the same way you always have.
(If students hesitate, use cues.)

Great job reading. Now let's go back to the first sentence and start over. This time, read all the sentences the fast way. Try the first one. I am Nat.

Repeat the process with the remaining sentences.

Individual Practice

(Provide individual practice with 1 sentence per student. Have students repeat the sentence until they can read smoothly.)

Excellent work today, everyone. You have worked together to earn a sticker for your Mastery Sheet.

I am Nat.

I am a ram.

Sam is a rat.

Sam and Nat sat on the mat.

131 Lesson 15

Fluency (Teacher's Edition A): Reading Story-Time Readers

Rebus Stories

The first type of **Story-Time Reader** is a rebus story. The text is composed totally of tricky words that have been previously introduced and pictures representing words. Rebus stories are used to transition students into reading books.

The steps for reading a rebus story are straightforward. Review tricky words with students, browse the book with students, and set the purpose for reading by having the students make a prediction. Read the title of the book in unison with students.

Then have students read the story in unison while you tap softly on the table, every four seconds, for each word or picture. After reading the story, check to see if your students' predictions came true. Review any missed words.

All **Story-Time Reader** activities end by providing individual practice with one or two pages per student. Rebus stories do not have fluency goals. During individual practice, students are encouraged to read as fast as they can without making errors. Students should read their individual pages until they can read the sentences smoothly and without error. Do not tap during individual practice.

ACTIVITY AT A GLANCE

- Step 1: Review tricky words.
- Step 2: Read the title of the book in unison with the students.
- Step 3: Browse the story, and set purpose by making a prediction.
- Step 4: Every four seconds tap softly on the table, once for each tricky word or picture your students read.

- Step 5: Review any missed words.
- Step 6: Check to see if students' predictions came true.
- Step 7: End with individual mastery check by providing practice with one or two pages per student. Do not tap during individual practice.

IN THE REAL WORLD

Check the rebus illustrations your students will have to identify before reading the rebus story. If any illustration is unclear, tell your students what word it represents, and then have them say the word together. For example, point to the illustration of the ball on page 3 of *A Table,* and say, **Students,** **this is a picture of a ball. Everyone, point to the picture. What is this a picture of?**

If time allows, challenge your students to read the sentence or the page that proves that their prediction was correct or to tell how the story differed from what they predicted.

Questions and Answers

(Review rules quickly.)
Sit tall.
Listen big.
Answer when I cue.
Answer together.

Activity 1
Part A: Tricky Words

Review

It's time to review all the tricky words we have learned so far.

(Use the Tricky Word Cards.)

(Hold up is.*) This word is* is. *Read it. is*

> **Repeat the process with the following tricky words: a, the, I, on, A, The, Is, have, are.**

(Shuffle the deck, and repeat the process with all the tricky words learned so far.)

Individual Practice

(Provide individual practice.)

Great job remembering the tricky words! We are now ready to read our story.

Part B: Story-Time Reader

Fluency Development

(Pass out Story-Time Reader 2, A Table.*)*

Note: Follow this format:
1. *Browse the story, and make a prediction.*
2. *Read the first page.*
3. *Students read the story in unison.*
4. *Check prediction.*

It's time to read. Put your finger on the title of the story.

The title of this story is *A Table.* What is the title of this story? *(Be sure students are following with their fingers.)* **A Table**

(Hold up a copy of the story, and turn the pages.) **Let's look at all the pictures in the story.**

(Allow time for students to browse the story.) **What do you think is going to happen in this story?** *(Have each student make 1 prediction.)*

Some of the words in this story are shown as pictures. When you see a picture, say the word that the picture stands for.
The rest of the words in this story are tricky words. That means when you see them, you say them fast. I will tap once for each word or picture. When I tap, read the word.

My turn to read first. *(Tap the table as you read each word to model.) (Tap.)* **A** *(tap)* **table**

Look at the next page. Now it's your turn to read. Remember to read the word when I tap so that you can read together. *(Tap.)* **A** *(tap)* **ball** *(tap)* **is** *(tap)* **on** *(tap)* **the** *(tap)* **table.**

(Proceed this way throughout the entire book.)

(Scaffold as necessary.)

(Restate the predictions.) **Did our predictions come true? What happened?** *(Discuss.)*

Individual Practice

(Provide individual practice with 1 page per student.)

Excellent job reading *A Table!* Now I can mark the Mastery Sheet.

123 Lesson 15

Story-Time Readers—Sounding-Out Format

After rebus stories are completed, the **Story-Time Readers** become fully decodable, meaning that all the words are composed of only previously taught letter-sound elements or tricky words. Initially students are taught to read tricky words fast but to sound out decodable words.

After sounding out the word, students then read the word fast. **/aaa/mmm/ *am*.** For this format, softly tap once for each sound, and then tell students, **Read it.** Tap once for each tricky word.

After students have sounded out and read each word in the sentence, they go back and read the sentence the fast way, following your auditory cue.

ACTIVITY AT A GLANCE

- Step 1: Review or preteach selected story words.
- Step 2: Students browse the story and make a prediction.
- Step 3: Students read the title of the story in unison.
- Step 4: Students read the story as you tap softly on the table, once for each tricky word, once for each sound in a decodable word, and then once to read that word. The maximum think time per word is specified in each reading activity.
- Step 5: After sounding out a sentence, students read the sentence fast.
- Step 6: Repeat the procedure with the remaining sentences on each page.

- Step 7: Students review any words they missed as they read the story. Write all the missed words on the marker board. Have students sound out each word to themselves, and then read the word fast. Then have the students read the list of missed words the fast way.
- Step 8: Discuss predictions with students.
- Step 9: Have students read the story a second time. This time they read the story fast, sounding out the words to themselves. Tap once for each word, allowing enough time between taps for students to sound out the decodable words to themselves. Start the timer with the first tap.
- Step 10: If a fluency goal is provided, start the timer, and have students read the book, taking turns reading one or two pages at a time for individual practice. Stop the timer when students have completed reading the entire chapter or book.
- Step 11: Review missed words.

IN THE REAL WORLD

If students are consistently struggling to meet their fluency goal, you need to assess the problem. Have they met mastery on the list of missed words before they read the story again? Do you need to slow the pace by allowing more think time between taps?

Questions and Answers

Activity 8
Story-Time Reader
Fluency Development

Language and Literacy Support

In this activity we will be reading a story called *Nan's Family.* I want to make sure you understand the story, so we are going to review a word.

The word is *scat.* Who knows what *scat* means? *(You may have to prompt students further by saying:)* Here is a hint. *If a cat is bothering me, I tell it to scat. (Accept reasonable responses.)*

That's right. *Scat* means "to move or to go away quickly."

Good job!

(Pass out Story-Time Reader 5, Nan's Family, to students. Have them turn to Chapter 1, "On the Mat.")

Note: Follow this format: Have students read from their books, pointing under the words as they read them. Tap once for each tricky word. Have students read tricky words fast, but have them sound out decodable words. Tap once for each sound in the word. After sounding out, have students say the word. Finally, have students read each sentence fast. Allow enough time between taps for students to sound out the decodable words. If students hesitate, use the following cues: "Read it" for tricky words, "Sound it out" for decodable words, and "Read it fast" after students sound out the sentence. Read the title to students, and then have students repeat the title with you.

Now let's read a new story, *Nan's Family.* When you see a tricky word, read it fast. How will you read tricky words? **fast**

Yes. For all other words, sound them out, and then say them fast. How should you read other words? **Sound them out.**

Yes. Then read the sentence fast.

(Have students browse the story and make predictions.)

The title of this chapter is *On the Mat.* Read the title of the chapter. *(Tap.)* On *(tap)* the *(tap)* /Mmm/ *(tap)* /aaa/ *(tap)* /t/. What word? *(Tap.)* **Mat.**

Read the title. *(Tap.)* On *(tap)* the *(tap)* **Mat.** Great. Now read the rest of the story. I will tap once for each sound to help you read together.

(Monitor to see that all students are pointing to the correct words.) Get ready. *(Pause. Tap.)* /D/aaa/d/ What word? *(Tap.)* **Dad**

(Follow the reading format outlined earlier for the entire story.)

Note: For the second reading, follow this format: Read the entire story the fast way. Tap once for each word, pausing 2–3 seconds between taps.

(Have students retell the story in sequence.) Now let's talk about what happened in the story.

Individual Practice

(Provide individual practice with each student reading one page the fast way.)

We have finished the lesson. You are doing a great job! I will put a check mark on the lesson Mastery Sheet.

Fluency (Teacher's Editions A, B, C): Story-Time Readers

Story-Time Readers: Fast First

Once students are reading stories by reading words fast first, story reading takes on a predictable set of steps. Building on research about the importance of repeated readings, each story is read multiple times. The objective is to read with increasing fluency on each subsequent reading.

ACTIVITY AT A GLANCE

- Step 1: Review or preteach selected story words.
- Step 2: Students browse the story and make a prediction.
- Step 3: Students read the title of the story in unison.
- Step 4: Students read the story as you tap softly on the table, once for each word. The maximum think time per word is specified in each reading activity. Start the timer with the first tap, and time the reading.

- Step 5: Review missed words.
- Step 6: Discuss predictions with students.
- Step 7: If students meet the fluency goal, move to individual practice. If the fluency goal is not met, students read the story in unison a second time. This time students read faster. After the second unison reading, complete individual practice. Time the individual practice, and record on the Mastery Sheet whether the group met the fluency goal.
- Step 8: Review missed words.

IN THE REAL WORLD

If an error occurs, have the students sound out the word together in a whisper voice, read the word fast, and then go back and reread the sentence.

Questions and Answers

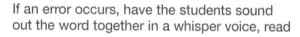

Activity 8

Story-Time Reader

Fluency Development

Language and Literacy Support (ELD)

During this activity we will be reading a story called *The Tin Man*. I want to make sure you understanding the story, so we are going to review a word.

The first word is *tin*. Who knows what tin is?

(You may have to prompt students further by saying:) **What do I mean if I say *The foil we use to wrap the food in is made with tin?*** *(Accept reasonable responses.)*

That's right. Tin is a type of metal. It is hard, not soft, and some things are made of it. In our story there is a tin man. He is made of tin. Here is a picture of the tin man. *(Show picture from Story-Time Reader 8, The Tin Man.)*

Excellent job!

*(Pass out **Story-Time Reader 8**, The Tin Man.)*

FLUENCY GOAL 44 words @ 20 words per minute (wpm) = 2 minutes, 20 seconds.

Note: Have students read from their books, pointing under each word as they read it. Students read in unison. Students read fast first. Tap once for each word, allowing enough think time between taps for students to sound out decodable words in their heads.

First Reading

(Have students browse the story and make predictions. Allow each student to make a prediction.)

For the last activity today, we are going to read a new story fast the first time. **How will you read?** fast the first time

If you know the word, say it when I tap. If you do not know a word, sound it out to yourself, and then say it fast when I tap. I will give you time to think before I tap. **Remember to point to each word in your book.**

Note: Provide no more than 5 seconds think time per word.

(Point to the first word in the title and say:) **I want you to read the title first. Everyone, point to the first word in the title of our story, and show me you are ready to read.** *(Monitor.)*

(Pause and tap.) **The** *(tap)* **Tin** *(tap)* **Man**

Good. Now let's read the first page. *(Pause, start the timer, and tap.)* **I**

Great! Now I want you to read the rest of the story. I will tap once for each word to help you read together. *(Monitor to verify all students are touching under the correct word.)*

Get ready. *(Pause and tap.)* **I**

Repeat the process with the entire story.

ERROR CORRECTION:
If students make an error, have students sound out the word in a whisper voice, read it fast, and then go back to reread the sentence. After each reading of the chapter, write the missed words on the marker board. Have students sound out each word in unison and then say it fast. Next have students read the list the fast way.

(Check students' predictions.)

294 Lesson 35

Lesson 35

Second Reading

Note: Provide no more than 4 seconds think time per word.

Now read the story again. Let's see if you can read it a little faster this time. Get ready.

(Pause, start the timer, and tap.)

Note: Review any missed words.

Individual Practice

(Call on individual students to read 1–2 pages. Do not tap during individual practice. Time students as a group. On the Mastery Sheet, note whether the group met the fluency goal.)

Retell

What happens first in this story? *(Call on students to retell the story in their words, 1 event at a time. Be sure every student retells at least 1 event.)*

Great job reading the story! We have finished our lesson for today, and you know what that means. I will mark the Mastery Sheet.

295 Lesson 35

Use of Auditory Cues

The auditory cue during group reading is a tool for controlling think time. To help students meet the fluency goals, tap softly on the table for each word read. Pausing between taps sets the pace at which the students read. The pause provides think time, which allows students enough time to figure out the unknown words while moving students through the text as fast as they can read without error. Taps must be predictable and consistent, like a metronome.

The amount of think time is listed within each reading activity, and the amount of time gradually decreases throughout the curriculum to support fluency development. Do not tap during individual practice. During individual practice, students read as fast as they can without making errors.

Story Reading Routine: Day 1

Students will usually read the same story for two days. The first day the group reads the story two or three times. First the group reads the story in unison. Control the pace by tapping softly to cue students to read the next word. Each lesson specifies the maximum allowable think time between taps if students are to achieve the fluency goal. However, if students can read faster than the specified rate, you may set a slightly faster pace.

Read the story in unison a second time only if the group struggled to meet the maximum allowable think time for each word and did not meet the fluency goal for the story on the first read. Also, if multiple errors occurred in the first reading, students should read the story again in unison. However, if the group easily met the fluency goal and made less than two errors as a group, you can skip the second reading and move directly to individual practice. Before rereading the story, write any missed words on the board, and have students sound out the words and read them fast. Repeat this process with each rereading of the story. The second time the group reads the story in unison, push the group to read a little faster. Again control the pacing with soft taps.

During individual practice, each student reads one or two pages, while the other students follow along by pointing to each word with their fingers. Be sure to time how long it takes the group to read the story, and then record on the Mastery Sheet whether the group met the fluency goal for the story.

Story Reading Routine: Day 2 (Teacher's Editions B and C)

On the second day of reading a story, students are expected to read the story with greater fluency than the day before. Time the group again, and record on the Mastery Sheet whether the group met the fluency goal. If the group reads the story within the specified time, move to the next activity. If students are struggling to meet the fluency goal, have them repeat the reading. However, before rereading you may choose to model sections of the text.

Challenge Stories (Teacher's Editions B and C)

Story-Time Readers are typically taught over two lessons. However, when the specified fluency goal is met by the group on Day 1, you are directed to have students read the challenge story on Day 2. **Challenge Stories** begin in **Teacher's Edition B.** These short, decodable stories are similar to the **Story-Time Readers,** and they provide students with additional generalized fluency and comprehension practice.

Partner Reading: Beat the Clock

In **Teacher's Edition C,** you are directed to conduct Partner Reading: Beat the Clock on the second day of reading a story. If students met the fluency goal in the previous lesson, Partner Reading: Beat the Clock is conducted first before moving to the challenge story. If the fluency goal was not met during the previous lesson, have the students read the story an additional time before completing Partner Reading: Beat the Clock. In this case, the challenge story is *not* read.

For Partner Reading: Beat the Clock, you will partner with one student. Switch partners each session. Have the remaining students partner with the student sitting next to them. Listen to your partner read the story. Students who are partnered take turns reading one page at a time from the same **Story-Time Reader.**

When conducting Partner Reading: Beat the Clock, tell all the students what the fluency goal is, and use a timer or a stopwatch. Students then read as fast and accurately as they can in order to read the entire story before time runs out. Record on the Mastery Sheet whether the student you partnered with met the fluency goal for the story.

Achieving Reading Fluency Goals

As students meet the fluency goals, they should be reading smoothly, with expression, and without errors. If students are consistently unable to meet their goals, there are several strategies available to assist them. First, make sure students are truly mastering the list of missed words before they read the story the second time. If students continue to make errors while they read the story, they are having difficulty transferring words in isolation into story text. In this instance, review the missed words again. Have students practice reading these words in the story itself. Then have students practice reading the sentence containing the missed word until they can read it smoothly and fluently.

You may need to slow the pace a little. Once students are reading smoothly and without error, pick up the pace. If the students are still having trouble meeting the fluency goals, you may need to go back and reteach selected activities that led up to the story. It may be that the students did not retain a certain letter-sound correspondence, word concept, or decoding skill and need reteaching.

Strand Five: Comprehension Strategies

Comprehension Strategy instruction develops your students' ability to process text strategically, to organize concepts and information for retrieval, and to monitor their understanding of the text. Comprehension activities are primarily conducted orally to take advantage of the students' receptive and expressive vocabularies. Occasionally you will be directed to write the students' responses on the board.

Before Reading

Browsing the story begins in **Teacher's Edition A** and continues through the entire curriculum. Before reading a story, students look at the pictures and briefly discuss what they think the story is about. Read the title with the students, and ask them to make predictions about the story. Then set the purpose for reading as reading to see if their predictions come true.

Preteach any story words that might be difficult for students (requires teacher judgment). Students then read the story to see if their predictions are right.

During Reading

During reading, observe whether students are listening to what they are reading. This can often be evidenced by their use of contextual clues to self-correct. If you suspect students are not following the storyline, you may briefly check comprehension.

After Reading

After reading, check the students' predictions. This holds students responsible for the material they have just read. They read to see if what they thought was going to happen does indeed occur. If the predictions do not come true, students should be able to tell you what does happen.

Comprehension Strategies (Teacher's Edition A)

The **Story-Time Reader** activities begin in Lesson 10. Comprehension strategies are introduced as soon as students begin to read the **Story-Time Readers.** Students learn to use Story Retelling and Sequencing as a basic, routine approach to organizing the information in the stories they read.

After Reading: Sequencing Information

The first after-reading comprehension strategy taught in **SRA Early Interventions in Reading** is Sequencing. Sequencing information in a story provides a simple organizational structure from which students are able to access information for more advanced comprehension tasks.

In the beginning, students retell anything they remember from the story. After a couple lessons, students are required to retell the events from the story in the order they occurred. Then the students transition to identifying the *main* events of the story in proper sequence.

Story Retell

Students learn to retell the story in their own words, relating each event in the order it happened. The overall retell should be brief, taking no more than one or two minutes.

ACTIVITY AT A GLANCE

- Step 1: After reading the story and reviewing missed words, have students retell the story in their own words, one event at a time, in the order the events occurred.
- Step 2: Prompt students: **What happens first?**
- Step 3: Prompt students: **What happens next?**

- Step 4: Repeat the procedure until the story has been completely retold.
- Step 5: Individual mastery is achieved by calling on one student to retell what happened first, then calling on another student to say what happened next, and so on, until all students have identified at least one story event.

IN THE REAL WORLD

Answers may need to be scaffolded. Students may get the events out of order. They may relate an event incorrectly or bring in information that wasn't in the story. They may leave out events. If they get events out of order, prompt students by asking, **Does that make sense? Could that have happened before this did?** If they leave out events, have them browse through the book to see if they can self-correct. Finally, if they are really unable to retell the events, go back, and reread the book one page at a time. **Say What is happening on this page?** After the students answer, tell them **Yes, and this is the first thing that happens in the story. Now let's see what happens next.** Repeat this procedure with each remaining page.

Questions and Answers

Activity 8
Story-Time Reader
Fluency Development

Language and Literacy Support

During this activity we will be reading a story called *The Tin Man*. I want to make sure you understanding the story, so we are going to review a word.

The first word is *tin*. Who knows what tin is?

(You may have to prompt students further by saying:) **What do I mean if I say *The foil we use to wrap the food in is made with tin*?** *(Accept reasonable responses.)*

That's right. Tin is a type of metal. It is hard, not soft, and some things are made of it. In our story there is a tin man. He is made of tin. Here is a picture of the tin man. *(Show picture from Story-Time Reader 8, The Tin Man.)*

Excellent job!

(Pass out Story-Time Reader 8, The Tin Man.)

FLUENCY GOAL 44 words @ 20 words per minute (wpm) = 2 minutes, 20 seconds.

Note: Have students read from their books, pointing under each word as they read it. Students read in unison. Students read fast first. Tap once for each word, allowing enough think time between taps for students to sound out decodable words in their heads.

First Reading

(Have students browse the story and make predictions. Allow each student to make a prediction.)

For the last activity today, we are going to read a new story fast the first time. How will you read? fast the first time

If you know the word, say it when I tap. If you do not know a word, sound it out to yourself, and then say it fast when I tap. I will give you time to think before I tap. Remember to point to each word in your book.

Note: Provide no more than 5 seconds think time per word.

(Point to the first word in the title and say:) **I want you to read the title first. Everyone, point to the first word in the title of our story, and show me you are ready to read.** *(Monitor.)*

(Pause and tap.) **The** *(tap)* **Tin** *(tap)* **Man**

Good. Now let's read the first page. *(Pause, start the timer, and tap.)* **I**

Great! Now I want you to read the rest of the story. I will tap once for each word to help you read together. *(Monitor to verify all students are touching under the correct word.)*

Get ready. *(Pause and tap.)* **I**

Repeat the process with the entire story.

ERROR CORRECTION:
If students make an error, have students sound out the word in a whisper voice, read it fast, and then go back to reread the sentence. After each reading of the chapter, write the missed words on the marker board. Have students sound out each word in unison and then say it fast. Next have students read the list the fast way.

(Check students' predictions.)

Second Reading

Note: Provide no more than 4 seconds think time per word.

Now read the story again. Let's see if you can read it a little faster this time. Get ready.

(Pause, start the timer, and tap.)

Note: Review any missed words.

Individual Practice

(Call on individual students to read 1–2 pages. Do not tap during individual practice. Time students as a group. On the Mastery Sheet, note whether the group met the fluency goal.)

Retell

What happens first in this story? *(Call on students to retell the story in their words, 1 event at a time. Be sure every student retells at least 1 event.)*

Great job reading the story! We have finished our lesson for today, and you know what that means. I will mark the Mastery Sheet.

295 Lesson 35

Comprehension Strategies (Teacher's Edition B)

The activities covered in the Comprehension Strategies Strand in **Teacher's Edition B** come from two categories of comprehension strategies: Sequencing Main Events and Story Grammar. These comprehension tasks focus the students on identifying the essential elements of the story: main characters, setting, problem, main events, and outcome.

Comprehension Strategies (Teacher's Edition B): Sequencing Main Events

In **Teacher's Edition B** students are asked to identify only the *main* events of a story in proper sequence. Eventually this skill will support students when they are learning to summarize.

ACTIVITY AT A GLANCE

- Step 1: Students identify and sequence *main* events of the story.
- Step 2: Prompt students, **What happens first?**
- Step 3: Prompt students, **What happens next?**
- Step 4: Repeat the procedure until all the main events have been listed in sequence.
- Step 5: Individual mastery is achieved by calling on one student to say what happens first, then calling on another student to say what happens next, and so on, until all students have identified at least one event.

IN THE REAL WORLD

Students may try to retell everything that happened in the story. Scaffold their understanding of the difference between main events and story details. You may need to use a real-life example. For instance, your students woke up this morning, they came to school, and then they will go home. These are the three main events of their day. In between, they do class work, eat lunch, and talk with their friends, but these are not the main events.

Questions and Answers

Lesson 65

Activity 8
Part A: Sequencing

Note: If students mastered sequencing during Lesson 64, they do not have to repeat it in this lesson. Have students read Chapter 1 of the challenge story *Where Is Matt?*

(Have the marker board ready.)

Now think about what we just read. Whom is the story mainly about? *(Call on individual students, and write the answers on the marker board. Answers will vary but should include something about Zack.)* **Zack**

Good. Let's continue. What happens first in the story?

> Repeat the process until students have listed all the events in the story.

You have all done a great job of reading and remembering this story.

TEACHER'S GUIDE

1. A man named Zack drives by in a bus.
2. Zack shows the children his big brass band.
3. Zack plays his band.
4. He is tired, so he gets back on the bus.

Part B: Challenge Story

- If time remains after completing Part A, have students read **Challenge Stories**, pages 29–36, "Where Is Matt?" Chapter 1.
- **Fluency Goal:** 56 words @ 32 wpm = 1 minute, 50 seconds
- Difficult words: *tuna, gingersnaps (Write the words on the marker board. Read the words to students. Have them try to read the words in the story. If students miss the words in the story, supply the words for them.)*
- Read the story title and chapter title to students.
- Have students browse the chapter and make predictions.
- After reading the pages in unison, give individual practice with 1–2 pages per student. The fluency goal does not have to be met for challenge stories.
- Write any missed words on the marker board and review the words with students.
- Review student predictions.
- Check for comprehension by having students retell in order the main events of the chapter.

Congratulations! You have done a terrific job completing this lesson, and you know what that means! I will mark the Mastery Sheet.

Comprehension Strategies (Teacher's Edition B): Story Grammar

Story Grammar organizes the major elements of a story into main character(s), setting, problem, main events, and outcome.

Story Grammar provides a framework for students to examine the connections between story elements, which leads to a deeper understanding of a story.

ACTIVITY AT A GLANCE

- Step 1: Write the following words in a column on the marker board: *Who; Where; Problem; Events: 1, 2, 3, 4, 5;* and *Outcome.*
- Step 2: Guide the students through each part. **Whom is this story mainly about?**
- Step 3: **Where does this story take place, or where does it mainly happen?**
- Step 4: **What does the main character want?**
- Step 5: **What does the main character do to solve the problem?**
- Step 6: **What happens in the end?**
- Step 7: Individual mastery is achieved by giving each student an opportunity to identify at least one major element of the story.

IN THE REAL WORLD

Story Grammar is a logical activity for students. They understand what you want from them. They may be challenged in identifying certain elements and might require scaffolding. Sometimes students want to identify every character in the story as the main character. If this occurs, you may say, **Yes, everyone you mentioned is in this story, but this story is mainly about one of them. Which character is the one with the problem?** Now, your scaffold has helped the students identify two of the major elements. Eventually students need to be able to access the relationship between all the major elements, so you want your scaffolding to support this relationship.

Questions and Answers

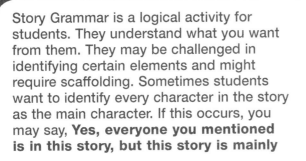

Lesson 70

Activity 2
Part A: Story Grammar

Note: In order to facilitate students' understanding of what they read, help them discover how the elements of a story are related. These elements bring organization and meaning to a student's comprehension of the story's message. Each of the story elements is defined as follows:

- **Main character**—whom or what the story is mainly about
- **Setting**—where and when the story happens
- **Problem**—what the main character must solve
- **Major events**—the most important things that happen to solve the problem
- **Story outcome or ending**—whether the problem is resolved

When discussing the story elements with students, it is important to do a lot of scaffolding, questioning, and prompting.

(Have the marker board ready.)

Note: Follow this format:

1. *Write the following words vertically on the marker board:* Who; Where; Problem; Events: 1, 2, 3, 4; Outcome.
2. Guide students through each part. Ask students, *"Whom is this story mainly about?" Explain that a story is usually about one main person. (Call on individuals to answer the main character question.) When a student gives the correct answer, say, "I will put* Chirp *and* Scat *next to* Who *because this story is mainly about them."*
3. Ask students, *"Where does this story take place?" Remind students that the setting is where the story takes place. When a student answers correctly, say, "Yes, the setting of our story is a house and a backyard. So I will write that next to* Setting *because that is where our story takes place."*
4. Ask students, *"Do* Chirp *and* Scat *have problems to solve?" When a student answers correctly, say, "Next to* Problem, *I will write* Chirp *doesn't want* Scat *in the house."*
5. Have students sequence the events. Remind students that the events are the most important things that happen to help Chirp and Scat solve their problems.
6. For Outcome, ask, *"What happens at the end of the story?" When a student answers correctly, say, "Yes,* Chirp *and* Scat *are friends."*

You have done a great job on this activity. Let's continue.

Part B: Challenge Story

- If time remains after completing Part A, have students read **Challenge Stories,** pages 37–44, "Stuck!" Chapter 2.
- **Fluency Goal:** 103 words @ 35 wpm = 3 minutes, 5 seconds
- Difficult words. *(Write any words that may be difficult for students on the marker board. Read the words to students. Have them try to read the words in the story. If students miss the words in the story, supply the words for them.)*
- Read the story title and chapter title to students.
- Have students browse the chapter and make predictions.
- After reading the pages in unison, give individual practice with 1–2 pages per student. The fluency goal does not have to be met for challenge stories.
- Write any missed words on the marker board, and review the words with students.
- Review students' predictions.
- Check for comprehension by having students retell in order the main events of the chapter.

228 Lesson 70

Comprehension Strategies (Teacher's Edition C)

The activities covered in the Comprehension Strategies Strand in **Teacher's Edition C** come from three categories of comprehension strategies: What I Know/ What I Learned, Main Idea, and Genre Identification. These are more advanced comprehension strategies that require students to compare and contrast and to draw inferences about what they are reading. Note that Language and Literacy Support appears frequently in Fluency and Comprehension activities, providing additonal scaffolding for students.

Comprehension Strategies (Teacher's Edition C): What I Know/What I Learned

What I Know/What I Learned is a comprehension strategy that appears in **Teacher's Edition C.** Make a chart to record student responses before and after reading a story: "What I Know" and "What I Learned." Discussing and recording what students already know about a topic prior to reading provides an organizational framework through which students can understand and recall more easily new information. Identifying new information they learned through reading deepens students' understanding of a selection.

ACTIVITY AT A GLANCE

- Step 1: Draw two columns on the marker board. On the left side write "What I Know." On the right side write "What I Learned."
- Step 2: Have students fill in the information they already know on the left.
- Step 3: Read the story.

- Step 4: Students report what they learned.
- Step 5: Summarize the information.
- Step 6: Individual mastery for comprehension is achieved by letting each student take a turn telling what he or she learned from a page in the story.

IN THE REAL WORLD

If your students are reluctant at first to provide information for "What I Know," or if they are prone to giving random answers, prompt them with questions that relate the topic to their lives. For example, when filling out the chart on the story *The Spider Club,* you might ask, **When's the last time you saw a spider? Where was it? Where outside do you think spiders live? So spiders might live outside in bushes and trees. Let's read the story and see if we learn where spiders live.**

Questions and Answers . . . .

Sometimes students may be very savvy about a particular topic, and you will have to limit the amount of information they give you. Limit each student to one or two answers. After reading the story, when you are completing "What I Learned," you can say, **You already knew this. You really do know a lot about spiders. What new information did you find out about spiders?** Always validate what students bring to the lesson. This builds their confidence and supports future learning.

Activity 6
Story-Time Reader
Part A: What I Know

(Pass out Story-Time Reader 45, The Spider Club, to students.)

The title of our new story is *The Spider Club*. Say the title with me.

(Teacher and students:) **The Spider Club**

(Browse the story. Let students comment on the pictures and make predictions. Have each student make a prediction.)

(Follow this format for the first part of the lesson: Write Spiders at the top of the marker board. Draw a vertical line to divide the marker board into 2 columns. At the top of the left column, write What I Know. At the top of the right column, write What I Learned. In the What I Know column, write the following words: Kinds, Eat, Live, and Body. Leave spaces between the words so you can fill in the information. Fill in the information on the marker board by asking students the following questions: "What kinds of spiders do you know? What do spiders eat? Where do spiders live? What do spiders look like?")

In this story, one of the main characters knows a lot about spiders. When you read this story, you will learn what she knows about spiders. *(Point to the marker board.)*

Before we find out what what she knows, let's find out what you already know about spiders. After we read the story, we will see if you learned anything new about spiders.

(Elicit responses, and write them under the What I Know column on the marker board. Do not erase the information in the What I Know column.)

Let's see what else we can learn about spiders from our story.

Look at the first page of the story. *(Pause, and monitor.)*

Read the title. *(Tap for each word.)* **The Spider Club**

Part B: Fluency Development

(ELD)

Language and Literacy Support

During this activity we will be reading a story called *The Spider Club*, and I want to make sure you understand all the words we will be reading.

The first word is branch. Who knows what a branch is? *(If students give another correct meaning, acknowledge it, but focus on the contextual meaning in the selection.)*

(You may have to prompt further by saying:) **Here's a hint. A bird sat on the tree branch.** *(Accept reasonable responses.)*

That's right. A branch is the part of a plant or tree that grows from the stem or trunk. Here is a picture of a branch. *(Show pictures from pages 2 and 3 of The Spider Club.)*

The next word is frame. Who knows what a frame is? *(If students give another correct meaning, acknowledge it, but focus on the contextual meaning in the selection.)*

(You may have to prompt further by saying:) **Here's a hint. We will put the mattress on a bed frame so the mattress does not fall.** *(Accept reasonable responses.)*

That's right. A frame holds up another object. A frame usually keeps the other object from falling. In the story, you will read how a spider spins special threads to create a frame for its web. This frame keeps the other threads from falling. *(Show pictures on pages 14 and 15 of The Spider Club. Point to the web's frame.)*

The next word is dine. Who knows what dine means? *(You may have to prompt further by saying:)* **Here's a hint. We wanted to dine at that restaurant, but it was closed.** *(Accept reasonable responses.)*

That's right. *Dine* means "to eat." Great job!

Lesson 94

Individual Practice

(Call on individual students to read 1–2 pages. Do not tap during individual practice. Time students as a group. Note on the Mastery Sheet whether the group achieved the fluency goal.)

FLUENCY GOAL 372 words @ 47 wpm = 8 minutes

We are going to read this story in a different way. Each of you will read by yourselves the first time. When I call on you, read as fast as you can without making mistakes. If you are not the one reading aloud, follow along and read to yourself. Point to each word. You may read to yourself in a soft whisper voice while following along.

(Call on the highest-achieving student to read first. Each child reads 1 page. Continue the rotation until the whole story has been read, making sure each student has an opportunity to read.)

(Follow the usual error correction process for Individual Practice. Review any missed words on the marker board. If an error occurs on a VCe word, remind students about the silent-e rule.)

Part C: What I Learned

(Review with students the What I Know information written on the marker board.)

Now turn back to the first page of the story. *(Monitor.)*

Reread this page to yourselves. *(Monitor, and pause long enough for students to reread the page.)*

What did we learn on this page? *(Answers will vary.)*

Good! *(Write the new information under What I Learned.)*

Repeat this process for each page in the story.

(Quickly summarize the new information for students.)

***The Spider Club* is a long story. You have done a great job reading and understanding this story. We are finished with our lesson, so I will mark the Mastery Sheet.**

Note: You will use the information for this activity in Lesson 96. Record the information so you can use it again.

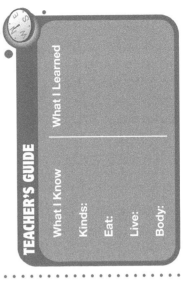

TEACHER'S GUIDE

What I Know	What I Learned
Kinds:	
Eat:	
Live:	
Body:	

Comprehension Strategies (Teacher's Edition C): Main Idea

The ability to identify the main idea allows the reader to identify the main theme of a story. Students often include unnecessary information when stating the main idea of a story. Often it can sound more like a brief summary of the story. The basic strategy to use is to ask students to first name whom or what the story is mainly about. Then ask students to talk about the most important thing they learned about who or what. The main idea of a story usually includes the main character, the problem, and its outcome.

ACTIVITY AT A GLANCE

- Step 1: Identify the main idea of the story.
- Step 2: **Whom or what is this story mainly about?**
- Step 3: **What is the most important thing we learned about the who or what?**
- Step 4: Students restate the main idea in as few words as possible.
- Step 5: Ask students, **Can we say that in fewer words?**

- Step 6: Pause to see if the students can restate the main idea in fewer words.
- Step 7: Model stating the main idea in very few words.
- Step 8: Have the students count the words.
- Step 9: Individual mastery is achieved if each student can demonstrate understanding of the main idea and can state it using only a few words.

IN THE REAL WORLD

This is a very challenging task for your students. They may need a lot of scaffolding. If students have difficulty in identifying the main idea, use the following process to assist them. Use *Story-Time Reader 49, Steve's Secret,* as an example. Ask whom or what the story is about. Answer: Steve. Then ask what is important to Steve. Answer: Steve has a secret. Finally, flesh out the main idea. Answer: Steve has a secret he doesn't want to share.

After your students identify the main idea in the story, they may include unnecessary details when they state the main idea. You will need to help students see which information needs to be left in and which information can be taken out. For example, Steve has a secret, and he is holding it behind his back, and he doesn't want to tell anyone what he has behind his back. You can take their own words and pull out the unnecessary information, thus restating the idea in fewer words. Steve has a secret, and he doesn't want to tell anyone. This is an acceptable restatement. Students can continue to work on stating the main idea in ten words or less for future stories. In the beginning, you need to let them know that you are looking for the most important information and nothing extra.

Questions and Answers

Activity 6
Main Idea

Let's talk about Steve's Secret.
What is this story mainly about? *(Discuss briefly.)*

Do you think we can say the main idea in fewer words? I think we can. *(Pause to see if students can restate the main idea in fewer words.)*

Now listen as I try. Count how many words I use. *(Monitor.)*
Steve has a secret he doesn't want to share.

Note: Follow this process for determining the main idea:

1. *Ask whom or what the story is mainly about.*
2. *Ask what is important about the main person, place, or thing in the story.*

Good job remembering our story. We have finished the lesson, and you know what that means!

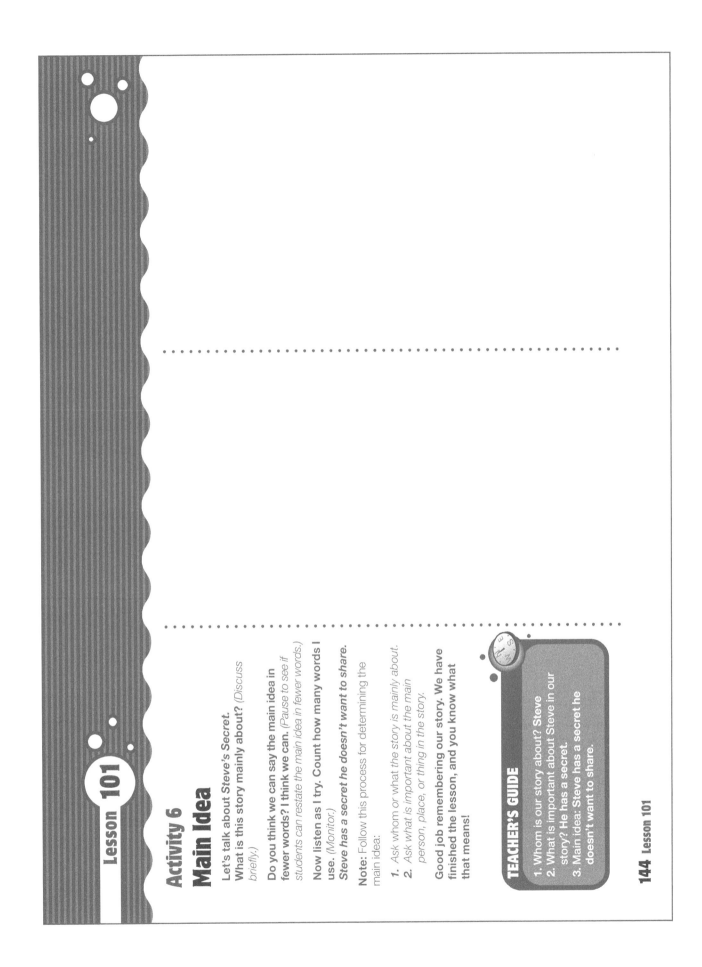

TEACHER'S GUIDE

1. Whom is our story about? **Steve**
2. What is important about Steve in our story? He has a secret. **He has a secret.**
3. Main idea: **Steve has a secret he doesn't want to share.**

144 Lesson 101

Comprehension Strategies (Teacher's Edition C): Genre

Students gain additional ownership of the material they read when they assess it for genre and underlying organizational structure. In **Teacher's Edition C,** your students will be exposed to real versus fantasy, absurdity, and satire. You are not teaching the specific genre. You are teaching the students to find the perspective and the reason the story was written.

ACTIVITY AT A GLANCE

- Step 1: After your students have read the story, discuss selected story events.
- Step 2: Ask leading questions that help students look more closely at the underlying structure of the story.

- Step 3: Individual mastery is achieved by making sure all students participate in the discussion and each student demonstrates knowledge of the story's genre.

IN THE REAL WORLD

Remember, you're not trying to teach your students specific genre; you are trying to get them into the habit of looking more closely at what they are reading and finding the perspective. With **Story-Time Reader 42,** Magic Pages, scaffold until the students understand that the trip is imaginary, not a trip to someplace real. Ask questions that get them to think about what they are reading: **Does the girl really climb on the backs of whales? Why do you think the book is called Magic Pages?**

Questions and Answers

Lesson 90

Activity 5
Part A: Comprehension

Real or Fantasy?

(Have students reread page 2 in Magic Pages.)

Everyone, turn back to page 2 in the book. Reread this page to yourselves, and then I will ask you some questions about it.

(Pause long enough for students to read the page.)

What does the girl mean when she says "I can take a trip"?

(Scaffold until students understand that the trip comes from reading stories, not from going somewhere real.)

Repeat the process for each page. Ask students questions such as "Does the girl really (do this)?", and then say, "Oh, she reads a story about (that)."

Now I will tell you what I think this story is mainly about. Tell me if you agree.

(Summarize the story for students.)

By reading stories, the girl can pretend to go to interesting places and to do many fun things.

Raise your hand if you think I have told you what the story is mainly about.

(Have students repeat what the story is mainly about.)

What a great job reading this story! I will mark the Mastery Sheet.

Part B: Challenge Story

- After students reach the fluency goal for the main selection, have them read *Challenge Stories*, pages 73–80, "Brave Liz," Chapter 2.
- **Fluency Goal:** 140 words @ 45 wpm = 3 minutes, 10 seconds
- Difficult Words: *(Write any words that may be difficult for students on the marker board. Read the words to students. Have them try to read the words in the story. If students miss the words in the story, supply the words for them.)*
- Read the story title and chapter title to students.
- Have students browse the chapter and make predictions.
- After reading the pages in unison, give individual practice with 1–2 pages per student. The fluency goal does not have to be met for challenge stories.
- Write any missed words on the marker board, and review the words with students.
- Review students' predictions.
- Check for comprehension by having students retell in order the main events of the chapter.

(Praise students, put a check mark on the Mastery Sheet, and move to the next activity.)

Guidelines for Teaching the First SRA Early Interventions in Reading Lesson

Activity 1: Rules

SRA Early Interventions in Reading Rules: It is important to begin by explaining the four rules: Sit tall. Listen big. Answer when I cue. Answer together. State the rule, and model the correct behavior. You may add additional rules at your own discretion. Some teachers like to add these two rules: Eyes up front. Watch me.

Cues: Tell the students that a cue is something you will do to tell them when to answer. Explain what types of cues you plan to use. Sometimes the activity will include instructions regarding what cue to use, but other times it will not. When the cue is not specified, you may select an appropriate cue. You may want to nod your head after asking a question students are supposed to answer. You may want to drop your hand after asking the question, or you may want to use a spoken cue after asking a question. The choice is yours, but consistency is essential to ensure students learn to watch for your cue and understand when to respond.

Merits of Becoming a Better Reader: Discuss with your students the merits of becoming a better reader. There are many reasons for wanting to become a better reader. Reading is fun; reading helps you to do your homework; reading helps you understand directions. Reading helps you learn about anything you are interested in, such as bikes, skateboards, sports, or music. Reading helps you know how to follow a recipe, how to put a model together, and learn other skills. Ask students for their ideas and reasons it is important to learn how to read well.

Mastery Sheet: Hold up the first Mastery Sheet, and show it to the students. Down the left column are the lesson numbers. One lesson is conducted each day. Within the lesson are several activities. Some lessons have six or seven activities; others might have eight, nine, or ten. You will place a check mark in the appropriate box after each activity is mastered. Once all the boxes are checked for the lesson, place a sticker in the last box to indicate that the students have mastered that lesson. You should show excitement about awarding the sticker at the end of a mastered lesson, because this indicates the students' success. If for some reason the lesson is not completed during the assigned time frame, start with the unfinished activity or activities before starting the next lesson.

Praise: When giving students positive feedback, remember to make it specific to their behavior. For example, say "Great job sounding out all those words," instead of just "Great job."

Activity 2: Rhyme Time

This activity presents two words, and you ask students if the words rhyme. After presenting the two words, signal for the unison response. Since this is the first lesson, practice unison responding if the group is having trouble responding together. This is the time to establish the correct response behavior. Students will be required to respond in unison throughout the entire **SRA Early Interventions in Reading** curriculum. If any students consistently make mistakes on whether the pair of words rhymes, back up and explain what it means for two words to rhyme. (They have the same ending sounds.) Then restart the activity.

Activity 3: First-Sound Game

In this activity, you will say a word, emphasizing the first sound in the word. You should hold the first sound for two or three seconds before saying the rest of the word. */Sss/un.* This helps the students hear the first sound. (The same procedure applies to later activities stressing the ending sound.) It is crucial that the sounds are held for an extended time if the students are going to benefit from this activity. Emphasizing the first sound allows the students to hear the separate phoneme in the word.

Activity 4: Letter-Sound Introduction

Use the Mm letter-sound card to introduce the sound of the letter *m.* Remember to hold the sound for at least two or three seconds. When you read the Muzzy the Monkey poem, stretch all the */mmm/* sounds. During the second reading, have the students say the */mmm/* part with you.

Activity 5: Thumbs Up—Thumbs Down Game: First Sound

This is an auditory activity in which the students listen to the first sound in a given word and determine whether the word begins with a specified letter-sound. (In this lesson the sound is */mmm/*.) As in Activity 3, you are instructed to emphasize the first sound in the word. This means you should hold the first sound for two or three seconds before saying the rest of the word. You should have the students practice putting their thumbs up, putting their thumbs down, and placing their hands flat on the table as they would between words.

Activity 6: Stretch the Word Game

When stretching words, it is very important that you do *not* stop between sounds. Each individual sound should blend into the next. It is equally important that you do *not* hold stop sounds, as this would distort the sound. Finally, it is imperative that you do *not* add any sounds to the end of stop sounds, as this would again be a distortion of the true sound. For example, the sound of the letter *b* is */b/* and *not /buh/.* When stretching words and using your visual cues, it is important that you do **NOT** mouth the sounds. Because this is the first time the students are being asked to perform this skill, it is important that they learn the procedures correctly. Take the time to train them on the correct visual cues, since they will be asked to perform this skill throughout the curriculum.

Activity 7: Writing the Letter

Review the letter formation guide in the Appendix of the **Teacher's Edition** before modeling how to form each letter. The students' letters should be legible; however, the activity should not be turned into a penmanship lesson. If your school has its own writing system, use that system when modeling letter formation.

When the dialogue directs you to demonstrate how to write a letter, model writing the letter on the marker board, on the chalkboard, or on a copy of the activity sheet.

Activity 8: Reading a Poem

The point of this activity is to teach the students about left-to-right orientation. We read words from left to right, so words run from left to right across the page. Point to each word as you read, and explain to students that pointing to words helps them not miss a word when reading. The finger pointing ensures speech-to-word matching so that they are reading the actual word to which they are pointing. This is particularly important when stories are reread. You need to continually monitor to make sure students are not just repeating what they have heard or read before.

You read the title first and then encourage students to make predictions on what the story might be about. Instruct students to listen carefully while the story is read so they can name words that begin with the /mmm/ sound. After reading the story, point to the word mouse, and say something like **Look, this word has the letter we just learned. What is this letter's sound?**

Using Language and Literacy Support

Language and Literacy Support is integrated into every lesson in the program, although it appears more frequently in the early lessons as students adjust to classroom routines and procedures. In Lesson 1, use the ELD support to clarify the meanings of cues, rhyming, mastery, stretching, and dots and dashes. Before reading the poem in Activity 8, explain the meanings of mouse and house, encouraging students to discuss the words and use them in sentences. Provide visual scaffolding with photographs in **Pictures for Language and Literacy, Level 1.**

The language and literacy supports are designed specifically to meet the needs of English language learners. However, they are appropriate for all students who struggle with oral language.

Concluding the Lesson

Be sure to check the Mastery Sheet after each activity has been completed. When the entire lesson has been mastered, let the students know how proud you are of them for doing such a great job. Be specific in your praise. For example: **Good job listening to the instructions! I like the way you are all answering together. You listened for the first sound in many words!** Place a sticker on the Mastery Sheet, collect materials, and move to the next lesson or dismiss students, as appropriate.

Lesson 1

Activity 1
Rules

Good morning! My name is _____. I am going to be one of your reading teachers this year.

Let's introduce ourselves. *(Take a few moments to learn each student's name and to let students greet each other.)*

Now that we know each other's names, we need to talk about a few things. We are going to be working together each day for reading. In order for you to become the very best readers, you have to learn some rules about how to behave when we work together.

Good. And what does a red traffic light signal people to do? stop

Excellent. In this class, I will use hand cues. I will use my hand to tell you what to do instead of saying it aloud.

When I give you a cue, it means I want you to answer together. What are you going to do when I do this? answer together

Yes. You will answer together. Good job!

(Explain and model each of the following rules. You may want to add other rules, such as "Eyes up front" or "Do your best.")

Sit tall.

Listen big. *(This means no talking until the teacher gives the cue.)*

Answer when I cue. *(Show students a few of your cues, such as holding up your hand like a stop sign or dropping your hand.)*

ELD
Language and Literacy Support

In this class, I will be using a cue to let you know when to answer. Does anyone know what a cue is? *(Accept reasonable responses.)*

That is right. A cue tells us something without using words.

Can anyone give me an example of a cue? *(You may have to prompt students further by saying:)* **What does a green traffic light signal people to do? go**

Answer together.

(Have students demonstrate each rule. You might need to prompt them by saying something like, "Show me sitting tall.")

When you work hard and follow these rules, you will become better readers. I expect you to follow these rules every day. If you follow these rules, we will finish our lessons, and you will become good readers.

(Discuss the merits of becoming a better reader. You might want to say, "Tell me why it is important to be a good reader." Explain the mastery measurement system and how students earn check marks and stickers on the lesson Mastery Sheets. Remember to praise students for following the rules throughout the rest of the lesson. Put a check mark on the lesson Mastery Sheet for this activity.)

Activity 2
Rhyme Time

ELD
Language and Literacy Support

Today we will be talking about rhyming words and doing activities with rhyming words. Does anyone know what rhyming means? *(Accept reasonable responses.)*

Yes, rhyming words are words that end the same. *(If all students seem to understand the definition, skip the following explanation.)*

For example, *bat* and *cat* both end with /at/. Another example is *man* and *tan*. Man and tan both end with /an/. Can anyone give me another example of two words that rhyme? *(Accept reasonable responses.)*

Yes, _____ and _____ do rhyme. *(If all students seem to understand the definition, skip the following.)*

No, _____ and _____ do not rhyme. *(If students make a mistake, stop, model the correct answer, have students say the correct answer with you, and then have them say the correct answer by themselves.)*

Mat *(pause)* fan. Do these rhyme? Yes. Stop. My turn. *(Point to self.)* Mat *(pause)* fan. Do these rhyme? No.

Say it with me. Mat *(pause)* fan. Do these rhyme? *(Teacher and students)* No. Your turn. (Point to students.) Mat *(pause)* fan. Do these rhyme? No.

Let's review one more time. What do we call words that end the same like bat and cat? rhyming words

That's right. Words that end the same like bat and cat are called rhyming words. Good job!

(This activity will help students answer together and on cue.)

Now we are going to do an activity called Rhyme Time. I'm going to say two words. Tell me if they rhyme.

I will do the first one. My turn.
Hat *(pause)* cat.
Do they rhyme? *(Use your cue, such as the hand drop.)* Yes.

Now it's your turn. I'll give you a cue, and you answer. *(Demonstrate cue.)* Remember to answer together when I cue.
Bell *(pause)* shell.
Do they rhyme? *(Pause, and cue.)* Yes.

Very good. Listen.
Man *(Pause.)* fan.
Do they rhyme? *(Pause, and cue.)* Yes.

Repeat the process with the following pairs of words: moon—mat, mouse—house.

Individual Practice
(Provide individual practice.)

Note: If students do not understand rhyme, tell them words rhyme if they have the same ending sound unit. For example, *bat—cat* have the same ending sound unit *-at. Fan—man—tan* have the same ending sound unit *-an.* If students make a mistake, implement the model-lead-test strategy. Stop students, and model the correct answer. Have students say the correct answer with you, and then have them say the correct answer by themselves.

ELD
Language and Literacy Support

Today I want to teach you a new word. The word is *mastery.* The sheets I mark when we finish a lesson are called Mastery Sheets. Can anyone tell me why? *(Accept reasonable responses.)*

That is a good idea. The word mastery comes from the word master. If you master something, you know it so well you do not have to think about it.

2 Lesson 1

If I mark on the Mastery Sheet, that means you have learned how to do what we are working on so well that I don't need to keep reviewing it with you.

What am I going to do if you do so well on an activity that you do not have to think about it? **mark on the Mastery Sheet**

That is right. If you know it so well that we do not need to review it anymore, I'll mark it on the mastery sheet. Good job!

Example: *Fan (Pause.) tan.* Do these words rhyme? **No.**
Stop. My turn. *(Point to yourself.) Fan—tan.* Do these words rhyme? **Yes.**

Do it with me. *Fan—tan.* Do these words rhyme? *(Teacher and students:)* **Yes.**

Your turn. *(Point to students.) Fan (Pause.) tan.* Do these words rhyme? **Yes.**

Excellent. I will mark the Mastery Sheet. That will let me know which parts of the lesson you have finished. Remember, we keep working on a part of a lesson until we do it perfectly. You did this part correctly, so we can go to a new part after I mark the Mastery Sheet. Good job!

3 Lesson 1

Activity 3
First-Sound Game

(Emphasize the first sound in the word when saying the word to students. Hold the sound 2–3 seconds so students can hear the first sound distinct from the rest of the word.)

Now we are going to do something different. I'll say a word. When I cue, tell me the first sound you hear in the word. This is the cue I will use. *(Demonstrate, holding up one finger.)* I'll do one first.

My turn. *Mmmouse.* **What is the first sound in *mouse*?** *(Hold up one finger.)* /mmm/ **Do you hear it? *Mmmouse.*** *(Pause.)* /mmm/

Listen for the first sound. Do it with me. *Mmmouse.* *(Pause.)* **What's the first sound you hear?**
(Teacher and students:) /mmm/
Yes, the first sound we hear in *mouse* is /mmm/.

Now it's your turn. I'll say a word. When I cue, you tell me the first sound you hear in the word. Remember to answer together on my cue. First word. */Sss/at.* *(Pause.)* **What is the first sound in *sat*?** *(Cue students by holding up one finger. This cue is related to the hand cue you will use in the stretching activities.)* /sss/

Yes, the first sound in *sat* is /sss/.
New word. */Mmm/om.*
What is the first sound in */mmm/om*? *(Cue students by holding up one finger.)* /mmm/
Next word.

Repeat the process with the following words: Ann, sip, me, map, soup, at.

(Scaffold as necessary. Use the model-lead-test strategy when a mistake is made.)

Individual Practice

(Provide individual practice with 2–3 words per student, and follow the directions in the Note below.)

Note:
1. **Individual Practice:** After students have answered in unison, many of the activities require individual practice. Always mix up the order when you call on students. They will pay more attention during individual practice if they don't know when you will call on them. Even though only one student is answering at a time, you want all students to listen, because this provides additional practice for all of them. Also, mix up the order of the words you give students so they do not memorize the answers without really knowing them.

2. **Praise:** When you give students positive feedback, make it specific to their behavior. For example, after the first sound activity you say, "Great job hearing the first sounds in those words!" instead of saying, "Great job." In other words, you want students to know exactly what it is they did correctly to earn the praise.

Great job hearing the first sounds in the words. You completed that game perfectly. I will mark the Mastery Sheet, and we can go to the next part of our lesson. (Give additional praise, such as "I like how all of you are sitting tall and paying attention.")

Activity 4
Letter-Sound Introduction

Language and Literacy Support

During this activity we will be reading a story, and I want to make sure that you understand the words from the story.

Who knows what yummy means? (You may have to prompt students further by saying:) **What do I mean if I say Pizza is yummy?** (Accept reasonable responses.)

That is right. Yummy means that it tastes good. (Demonstrate by rubbing your stomach.)

The next word is tummy. Does anyone know what tummy means? (You may have to prompt students further by saying:) **What do I mean if I say My tummy hurts?** (Accept reasonable responses.)

Yes. Your tummy is your stomach. (Demonstrate by touching your stomach.)

The last word is munch. Does anyone know what munch means? (You may have to prompt students further by saying:) **Here is a hint: The boy munched an apple.** (Accept reasonable responses.)

Yes. To munch is to chew something. (Demonstrate by pretending to munch an apple.) **Good job!**

When we read, we use letters to help us figure out words. Each letter stands for a sound. We are going to learn the sounds that letters stand for so you can use them to help you figure out words. Here is your first one. (Hold up the **Mm** letter-sound card. Point to M.)

This letter's sound is /mmm/. Say it with me.
(Teacher and students:) **/mmm/**
Again. Say it with me.
(Teacher and students:) **/mmm/**
Your turn. What sound? **/mmm/**

Lesson 1

Individual Practice

(Ask each student individually.)

Good. I am going to read a poem about /Mmm/uzzy the /Mmm/onkey. What is the first sound you hear in /Mmm/uzzy? (Cue students by holding up one finger.) **/mmm/**

We know that (point to m) this is the first letter we see in the word /Mmm/uzzy. Listen again. What is the first sound you hear in /Mmm/onkey? (Cue students by holding up one finger.) **/mmm/**

Right. Now we know (point to m) this is the first sound we hear in the word /Mmm/onkey.

Here is a poem about Muzzy the Monkey. This poem has many words with the /mmm/ sound.

Listen big so you can hear them. I will ask you about them after I read the poem. (Read the poem about Muzzy the Monkey. Emphasize the words with /mmm/ at the beginning.)

For Muzzy the Monkey, bananas are yummy.
She munches so many, they fill up her tummy.
When she eats, she says
/m/ /m/ /m/ /m/ /m/.

Bananas for breakfast, bananas for lunch.
Mash them up, mush them up,
munch, munch, munch.
When she eats, she says
/m/ /m/ /m/ /m/ /m/.

Bananas at bedtime? I have a hunch
She'll mash them and mush them
And munch, munch, munch.
Then what will she say?
When she eats, she says
/m/ /m/ /m/ /m/ /m/.

(Read the poem a second time, and have students say the /m/ /m/ /m/ part with you. Say, "I will read the poem again, and you say the /m/ /m/ /m/ part with me. What does Muzzy say?")

Who can tell me some words from the poem that had the /mmm/ sound in them?

(Hold up the **Mm** letter-sound card. Point to M.)

Everybody, what is this letter's sound? **/mmm/**

(Point to the monkey picture.) Here is a picture of **Muzzy the Monkey.** She is here to remind you about this letter's sound.

(Place the card on the table so students can see it during the remainder of the lesson.)

Good. We have finished another part of the lesson, so I will put a check mark on the Mastery Sheet for this activity, and we can move to the next part. You are doing a great job of listening, sitting tall, and answering together. Let's keep working.

Activity 5
Thumbs Up—Thumbs Down Game

First Sound

(ELD) Language and Literacy Support

Who knows what we call this finger in English? *(Hold up your thumb.)* thumb

That is right. We call it a thumb. *(If all students seem to understand the definition, skip the following.)*

How many thumbs do we have on our bodies? two

That is right. We have two thumbs. I tried to trick you because I know that sometimes in Spanish we call the big toes and big fingers the same thing, which would mean that we would have four.

However, in English the ones on our hands are called thumbs and the ones on our toes are called "big toes," not thumbs.

What are you going to do if I ask you to put your thumbs up? *(Students should give a thumbs-up.)*

5 Lesson 1

Lesson 1

That is right. You'll put your thumbs up, like this. *(Give students a thumbs-up.)* Good job!

It's time for a new game. I am going to say a word. You listen to hear if it begins with this letter's sound. *(Point to m on card.)* What sound will you listen for? /mmm/

Right. Listen for /mmm/. Here's how we'll play this game. After I say a word, give me a thumbs-up if the word begins with the sound /mmm/. *(Demonstrate a thumbs-up.)*

Show me what you will do if you hear /mmm/ at the beginning of the word. *(Students should put their thumbs up.)* Show me how you put your thumbs up. *(Monitor, and correct.)*

If you do not hear the /mmm/ sound, give me a thumbs-down. *(Demonstrate a thumbs-down.)*

Show me what you will do if you do not hear /mmm/ at the beginning of the word. *(Students should put their thumbs down.)* Show me how you put your thumbs down. *(Monitor, and correct.)*

Optional: To prevent students from copying each other, you may want to have them put down their heads or close their eyes. Say, "There is one more part to this game. When we start, I want you to (put your heads down on the table OR close your eyes). Then I want you to rest your hands flat on the table until I say the first word."

Show me *(heads down OR eyes closed).* Keep your hands flat. *(Monitor, and correct.)*

Great job. Everyone is in the right position for this game. Ready. Listen. /Mmm/e. Do you hear /mmm/ at the beginning of /mmm/e? *(Students put their thumbs up.)*

(Monitor, and correct.)

Right. We do hear /mmm/ at the beginning of *me.*

Hands flat. Next word. *(Stretch the first sound in each word.)*

> **Repeat the process with the following words: see, my, sigh, meal, marble, beat, meet, moon.**

(If a mistake is made, immediately stop. Say:) **Stop. Listen.**

(Repeat the word, and ask:) **Cookie. Do I hear /mmm/ at the beginning of cookie? No, so I will put my thumb down.**

Do it with me. Cookie. Do you hear /mmm/ at the beginning of cookie? *(Check to be sure all thumbs are down.)*

Now by yourselves. Cookie. Do you hear /mmm/ at the beginning of cookie? *(Check to be sure all thumbs are down.)*

Good job! *(If using the option, tell students to put their heads up OR open their eyes.)*

Individual Practice

(Provide individual practice with 1–2 words per student.)

Excellent job listening for the /mmm/ sound at the beginning of words! You have done another great job, and you know what that means. I'll check off this section on the Mastery Sheet, and we will go to our next activity.

Activity 6
Stretch the Word Game

Language and Literacy Support (ELD)

(Have a rubber band ready.) **Who knows what *stretching* means?** *(You may have to prompt students further by saying:)* **What are we doing if we stretch a rubber band?** *(Accept reasonable responses.)* **Yes. When you stretch something, you pull it and make it longer.**

I have a rubber band. Watch how I stretch it. *(Stretch a rubber band.)* **Imagine you have a rubber band and you are pulling it. Do it with me.** *(Stretch a rubber band.)*

We can do the same thing with words. We can say them normally, or we can stretch them and make them sound longer. For example, if we stretched the word sun, we would separate each sound in the word like this: *(Be sure to emphasize that you are stretching the sounds. Don't chop them.)* **/S/ /u/ /n/.**

Do it with me. Keep stretching the sounds. While you stretch, I will stretch the rubber band so you can see how long to stretch the sounds.

Answer together: /s/ /u/ /n/ *(Stretch the rubber band until students finish answering.)*

Good. Who can tell me what stretching means? pulling something and making it longer

Yes. When you stretch something, you pull it and make it longer. Good job!

Here is a new game. It's called Stretch the Word. Here is how we play Stretch the Word. I'll say a word, and you will tell me the sounds you hear in the word. Watch how I do it. First I hold up my fist. *(Demonstrate.)* **Next I slowly say each sound I hear in a word, and I hold up one finger as I say each sound.**

My turn to do to the first word. Am. I'll stretch am. *(Hold up one finger for a and a second finger for m.)* **/Aaa/mmm/.**

Did you hear how I said each sound slowly, and did you see how I held up one finger for each sound?

Now stretch the word *(pause)* **am** *(pause)* **with me. Hold up your fist. Good. Am.** *(Pause.)* **Stretch am.** *(Teacher and students:)* **/aaa/mmm/**

Excellent! Now stretch by yourselves. Am. *(Pause.)* **Stretch am.** *(Use hand cues to guide students, but do not speak.)* **/aaa/mmm/**

(Practice until all students can stretch am, following your finger cue as a group.)

Individual Practice

(Check students individually. Be sure they are correctly using the hand cues.)

Here is a new word to stretch. My turn. I'll stretch *(pause)* **me.** *(Demonstrate.)* **/Mmm/eee/.**

Together. *(Pause.)* **Me.** *(Pause.)* **Stretch me.** *(Teacher and students:)* **/mmm/eee/**

Now by yourselves. Me. *(Pause.)* **Stretch me. /mmm/eee/**

(Practice until all students can stretch me, following your finger cue as a group. Be sure each student is using the hand cues correctly.)

Here is one more word to stretch. We will do this one together. See. *(Pause.)* **Stretch see.** *(Teacher and students:)* **/sss/eee/**

Now by yourselves. Stretch see. /sss/eee/

(Practice until all students can stretch see, following your finger cue as a group. Be sure each student is using the hand cues correctly.)

Note: Continue to use hand cues, even when it is the students' turn to stretch a word. The hand cues serve two functions. First, they keep students answering in unison, and, second, they cue students when to switch from one sound to another. This is very important. Students should not switch to the next sound until you raise your next finger.

You have done another part of the lesson perfectly. I'll check off this section on the Mastery Sheet.
Just two more parts, and we are finished with the whole lesson!

Optional: Some teachers have found that using a spring toy, such as a Slinky, helps students understand the concept of stretching a word. When the spring toy is stretched apart, it is still a spring toy. When students say the word slowly, it is like pulling the spring toy slowly. When students say the word at the normal rate, it is like putting the spring toy together again. Either way, it is still the same spring toy.

Activity 7
Writing the Letter

ELD

Language and Literacy Support

During this activity we will be writing, and I want to make sure that you understand everything I am talking about.

Who knows what a dot is? (You may have to prompt students further by saying:) **If I were to put a spot on your hand with this marker, what would that spot be?** (Accept reasonable responses.)

That is right. A dot is a small spot or point, like this: (Demonstrate drawing a dot on the marker board.)

What about a dash? Does anyone know what a dash is? (You may have to prompt students further by saying:) **If I drew a short line on the marker board, what would it be?** (Accept reasonable responses.)

Yes. A dash is a short line, like this: (Demonstrate drawing a dash.)

Good. Here's the last question: What does it mean if I tell you to trace something? (You may have to prompt further by saying:) **What if I tell you to trace the lines?** (Accept reasonable responses.)

Yes. To trace means to copy by connecting the dots or dashes, like this: (Demonstrate by drawing an O with dashed lines on the marker board and then tracing it.)
Excellent.

(Hold up the **Mm** letter-sound card. Point to M.)

What is this letter's sound? /mmm/

Yes, /mmm/. We are going to learn how to write the letter that makes the /mmm/ sound. Watch how I write it. (Model, explaining each stroke you make. Use the marker board and refer to the letter formation guide in the back of the book.)

(Have students turn to page 1 of **Activity Book A.**) **On the activity sheet, the letters are almost finished. Put your pencil on the big dot of the first letter.** (Demonstrate, and monitor.)

Let's trace that letter together. (Talk students through each pencil stroke. Have students say the /m/ sound as they trace and write the letter in this activity.)

Good job writing the letter that says /mmm/. Trace the next letter by yourselves. Say the /mmm/ sound while you trace it. Trace it fast. Trace it neatly. No erasing. (Monitor, and correct as necessary.)

(Have students trace all the m's on the first line.)

Good job tracing the letter that says /mmm/. Now let's write the letter that says /mmm/. Touch the first big dot. Write the letter. Make the sound of the letter while you write it. *(Monitor.)*
Put your pencil on the next dot. Write the letter. Say the /mmm/ sound while you write the letter.

(Have students finish all the m's on the second line.)

On the next lines, we will play a game. I'm going to say a word. If it begins with /mmm/, you will write the letter for /mmm/. Listen big. *(Pause.)* **Mouse. Do you hear /mmm/ at the beginning? Yes. Then write the letter for /mmm/. Start with the first dot.** *(Monitor.)*

Next word. Sat. Do you hear /mmm/ at the beginning? No. Will you write anything? No.

Good job. New word. Monkey. Do you hear /mmm/ at the beginning? Yes. Good. Write it in the second space. *(Monitor, and correct if necessary. Students will fill all the spaces.)*

Repeat the process with the following words: baby, mat, sat, mop, Muzzy, man.

(Praise students, and mark the lesson Mastery Sheet.)

9 Lesson 1

Activity 8
Reading a Poem
Read Aloud: If I Were a Mouse

ELD

Language and Literacy Support

During this activity we will be reading a poem, and I want to make sure that you understand the words from the poem.

The first word is mouse. Who knows what a mouse is? *(You may have to prompt students further by saying:)* **Here is a hint. A mouse was running in a field.** *(Accept reasonable responses.)*

That is right. A mouse is a small, furry animal. Here is a picture of a mouse. *(Hold up Pictures for Language and Literacy Support, page 1.)*

The next word is house. Does anyone know what a house is? *(You may have to prompt further by saying:)* **What do I mean if I say We moved into a new house?** *(Accept reasonable responses.)*

Yes. A house is a building where people live. Here is a picture of a house. *(Hold up Pictures for Language and Literacy Support, page 2.)*

The last word is friend. Who knows what friend means? *(You may have to prompt further by saying:)* **What do I mean if I say My friends and I ride bikes after school?** *(Accept reasonable responses.)*

Yes. Friend means someone you like to spend time with. The people you do things with, like playing games and sharing toys, are your friends. Good job!

(The poem for this activity appears on the next page.)
(There are three reasons for reading this poem.)
1. To demonstrate left-to-right orientation while reading
2. To model how to place the pointer finger under each word as the word is being read
3. To highlight the word mouse and explain that it begins with the letter-sound students have learned

The title of this poem is "If I Were a Mouse." Tell me what you think the poem will be about. *(Anything about being a mouse is acceptable.)*

You are right. This is a poem about what you would do if you were a mouse. I want you to watch how I point to each word as I read this poem. Pointing helps me stay on the right line and helps me so I don't miss any words. Follow my finger as I read. *(Hold up the book, and read the poem on the next page. Place your finger under each word as you read it.)*

(After you have finished the first reading, go back to the word mouse.)

Look. This word has the letter we just learned. What is this letter's sound? /mmm/ Very good. Now I will read the poem again. Follow my finger.

(Read the poem again, following the same pointing procedure as described for the first read.)

We have finished all the parts of our lesson. Do you know what that means? It means I can put a sticker on your lesson Mastery Sheet!

(Put a sticker on the lesson Mastery Sheet, provide praise, and put away materials.)

10 Lesson 1

Name _____

Lesson 1

_____

m

_____

Activity 7

m	m
m	m m

m   m   m

m   m   m

Activity Book A   1

Sample Lessons

On the following pages are three sample lessons, one from each **Teacher's Edition:**

Teacher's Edition A: Lesson 15
Teacher's Edition B: Lesson 71
Teacher's Edition C: Lesson 101

These lessons demonstrate the integration and progression of skills throughout the curriculum.

Notes
. . . .

MATERIALS

1. *Tricky Word Cards*
2. *Story-Time Reader 2, A Table*
3. Letter-Sound Card 8 (Ff)
4. Maxwell!
5. *Activity Book A,* page 19
   ELD *Pictures for Language and Literacy Support,* page 12

OBJECTIVES

Activities 1 and 9 *Fluency*
- Learn to write and automatically recognize irregular words in stories
- Demonstrate the ability to decode text and read words fast

Activity 2 *Letter-Sound Correspondences*
ELD Preview words from a poem
- Learn the sound of the letter *f*
- Associate sounds with letters
- Listen for and identify the /f/ sound in a poem

Activity 3 *Phonemic Awareness*
- Identify the position of a sound in a word

Activity 4 *Letter-Sound Correspondences*
- Associate sounds with letters

Activity 5 *Phonemic Awareness*
- Segment spoken words into sounds, and then say words

Activity 6 *Letter-Sound Correspondences*
- Learn the correct strokes for writing lowercase and capital letters
- Match the sounds of letters to printed letters

Activity 7 *Letter-Sound Correspondences*
- Identify letter-sounds, and write the letters for the sounds

Activity 8 *Word Recognition and Spelling*
- Segment words into phonemes, and then blend the phonemes to say words

(Review rules quickly.)
Sit tall.
Listen big.
Answer when I cue.
Answer together.

Activity 1

Part A: Tricky Words

Review

It's time to review all the tricky words we have learned so far.
(Use the Tricky Word Cards.)

(Hold up is*.)* This word is *is.* Read it. *is*

> Repeat the process with the following tricky words: **a, the, I, on, A, The, Is, have, are.**

(Shuffle the deck, and repeat the process with all the tricky words learned so far.)

Individual Practice

(Provide individual practice.)

Great job remembering the tricky words! We are now ready to read our story.

Part B: Story-Time Reader

Fluency Development

(Pass out Story-Time Reader 2, A Table*.)*

Note: Follow this format:
1. Browse the story, and make a prediction.
2. Read the first page.
3. Students read the story in unison.
4. Check prediction.

It's time to read. Put your finger on the title of the story.

The title of this story is *A Table.* What is the title of this story? *(Be sure students are following with their fingers.)* **A Table**

(Hold up a copy of the story, and turn the pages.) **Let's look at all the pictures in the story.**

(Allow time for students to browse the story.)
What do you think is going to happen in this story? *(Have each student make 1 prediction.)*

Some of the words in this story are shown as pictures. When you see a picture, say the word that the picture stands for.

The rest of the words in this story are tricky words. That means when you see them, you say them fast. I will tap once for each word or picture. When I tap, read the word.

My turn to read first. (*Tap the table as you read each word to model.*) (*Tap.*) **A** (*tap*) **table** (*tap*) **ball** (*tap*) **is** (*tap*) **on** (*tap*) **the** (*tap*) **table.**

Look at the next page. Now it's your turn to read. Remember to read the word when I tap so that you can read together. (*Tap.*) **A** (*tap*) **ball** (*tap*) **is** (*tap*) **on** (*tap*) **the** (*tap*) **table.**

(*Proceed this way throughout the entire book.*)

(*Scaffold as necessary.*)

(*Restate the predictions.*) **Did our predictions come true? What happened?** (*Discuss.*)

Individual Practice

(*Provide individual practice with 1 page per student.*)

Excellent job reading *A Table!* **Now I can mark the Mastery Sheet.**

Activity 2
Letter-Sound Introduction

ELD

Language and Literacy Support

During this activity, we will be reading a poem, and I want to make sure you understand the words from the poem.

The first word is *fan.* **Who knows what fan means?** (*You may have to prompt students further by saying:*) **What do I mean if I say** *We turned on the fan?* (*Accept reasonable responses.*)

That's right. A fan blows air to cool you off. (*Demonstrate by fanning yourself.*) **Here is a picture of a fan.** (*Show Ff Letter-Sound Card.*)

The next word is *fox.* **Does anyone know what a fox is?** (*You may have to prompt students further by saying:*) **What do I mean if I say** *There was a fox outside the chicken pen?* (*Accept reasonable responses.*)

Yes. A fox is a small wild animal a little like a wolf or a dog but smaller, with shorter legs. Foxes have large ears and bushy tails. Here is a picture of a fox. (*Hold up Pictures for Language and Literacy Support, page 12.*)

The last word is *whir.* **Does anyone know what whir means?** (*You may have to prompt students further by saying:*) **What do I mean if I say** *Fans whir in windows on hot summer days?* (*Accept reasonable responses.*)

Yes. Whir is a quiet sound. An electric fan makes a whirring sound. Whirring sounds like this. (*Demonstrate by rolling your tongue.*)

Good job.

(*Hold up the Ff letter-sound card.*)

This letter's sound is /fff/. Say it with me. (*Teacher and students:*) **/fff/ Again. Say it with me.** (*Teacher and students:*) **/fff/ Your turn. What sound? /fff/**

Individual Practice

(*Ask each student individually.*)

Good job. I am going to read a poem about Franny the Fan. Listen. I will stretch the beginning of the word *Franny.* **/Fff/ranny. What is the beginning sound you hear in the word /Fff/ranny? /fff/**

Yes. The beginning sound in *Franny* is /fff/. Good listening. Listen again as I stretch the beginning of the word *fan*. /Fff/an. What is the beginning sound you hear in the word /fff/an? /fff/

That is right, so we know (*point to f*) this is the first letter we hear in *Franny* and *fan*.

Here is a poem about Franny the Fan. This poem has many words with the /fff/ sound. Listen big so you can hear them. I'll ask you about them after I read the poem.

(*Read the poem, emphasizing the /fff/ /fff/ /fff/ sounds. Hold each individual sound 2 seconds.*)

/fff/ /fff/ /fff/ /fff/—What's that funny sound?
It's Franny the Fan going round and round.
And this is the sound that old fan makes:
/fff/ /fff/ /fff/ /fff/ /fff/.

When it gets too hot, you see,
Franny cools the family: /fff/ /fff/ /fff/ /fff/.
She fans Father's face,
And Foxy's fur,
And Felicity's feet.
Hear the fan whir: /fff/ /fff/ /fff/ /fff/ /fff/.

Can you make Franny the Fan go fast? (*Have students say quickly:*) /fff/ /fff/ /fff/ /fff/ /fff/
Faster? /fff/ /fff/ /fff/ /fff/ /fff/ /fff/
Fastest? /fff/ /fff/ /fff/ /fff/ /fff/ /fff/

What words did you hear with the /fff/ sound? (*Discuss.*)

(*Hold up the **Ff** letter-sound card. Point to* f.) Everybody, what is this letter's sound? /fff/

Ff

(*Point to* F.) What is this letter's sound? /fff/
(*Put the letter-sound card on the table for students to see.*)
Here is a picture of Franny the Fan. She is here to remind you of this letter's sound.

Great job saying /fff/. What should I do now? (*Encourage students to tell you to check off the activity on the Mastery Sheet.*)

Activity 3
Thumbs Up—Thumbs Down Game

Beginning or End

Now let's play the Thumbs Up—Thumbs Down game. I will say some words that may have the /fff/ sound.

After I say each word, I will cue. When I cue, put your thumbs up if the word has the /fff/ sound.

If the word does not have the /fff/ sound, put your thumbs down.

Listen as I do the first one. (*Emphasize the /fff/ sound in each example.*) /Fff/unny. (*Pause.*) Do you hear the /fff/ sound in /fff/unny? (*Give a thumbs-up.*)

Your turn. Listen carefully. /Fff/ast. Do you hear the /fff/ sound in /fff/ast? (*Students should give a thumbs-up.*)

Next word. Sa/fff/e. Do you hear the /fff/ sound in sa/fff/e? (*Students should put their thumbs up.*)

> Repeat the process with the following words: **fancy, stiff, family, life, leaf.**

Individual Practice

(Provide individual practice with 1–2 words per student.)

Good job hearing the */fff/* **sound. I will mark the Mastery Sheet so we can go to our next activity.**

Activity 4
Letter-Sound Review

It is time to review all the sounds we have learned so far. When I touch under a letter, say its sound. Keep saying the letter's sound for as long as I touch under the letter.

(Touch under n on the next page.) **What sound?** */nnn/*

(After the first row, say:) **The rest of the letters do not have dots. Say their sounds the way you always have.**

(Vary the time you touch under each letter 2–4 seconds to create a gamelike quality. Be quick with the stop sounds. Tell students that even when there are no arrows or dots, they will say the sounds like they have before.)

ERROR CORRECTION:
Oh, you let me trick you!
My Turn *(Say sound for 2 seconds.)*
/Together/Your Turn
(Back up 2 items.)

Individual Practice

(Provide individual practice.)

Great job remembering all the sounds we have learned. You have finished another activity perfectly. I will put a check mark on the lesson Mastery Sheet.

s

n

·

·

t

·

a

n

d

n

r

m

r

d

Activity 5
Stretch and Blend

(Place Maxwell the puppet on the table.)

It is time to teach Maxwell to speak. First I will say a word. Then you will stretch the word, holding up one finger for each sound you hear. Then say the word the fast way.

(Hold up your fist to demonstrate.)

Fists up. (Pause.) The first word is *fat*. (Pause.) Stretch *fat*. /fff/aaa/t/ What word did you stretch? fat

Next word. *Fast*.
Stretch *fast*. /fff/aaa/sss/t/ What word did you stretch? fast

Repeat the process with the following words: fist, fit, fits, ramp.

Individual Practice

(Provide individual practice.)

Excellent job stretching. You have earned another check mark.

127 Lesson 15

Lesson 15

Activity 6
Writing the Letter

(Have the Ff letter-sound card ready. Have students open their activity books to page 19. Allow no more than 4 seconds to write each letter.)

(Hold up the Ff letter-sound card. Point to f.)
What is this letter's sound?
/fff/

Now we are going to learn how to write the letter that stands for the /fff/ sound. Watch how I write it. *(Model, explaining each stroke you make. Use the letter formation guide at the back of this book.)*

On the activity sheet, the letters are almost finished. Put your pencil on the big dot of the first letter. *(Demonstrate, and monitor.)*

Let's trace that letter together. *(Walk students through each pencil stroke. Have students say the /f/ sound as they trace the letter and write it on their own in this activity.)*

Good job tracing the letter that says /fff/. Trace the next letter fast. Trace it by yourselves.
(Monitor, and correct as necessary.)

(Have students trace all the f's on the first line.)

Good job tracing the letter that says /fff/. Now let's write the letter that stands for the /fff/ sound. Touch the big dot of the first letter, and trace it. Say the /fff/ sound as you neatly write the letter f.

(Have students complete all the f's on the second line.)

Good job writing the letter that says /fff/. Now you are going to write the letter that says /fff/ by yourselves. Write the letter three times. *(Point to the line on which students will write their f's. Remind students to softly say the /fff/ sound as they write the letters.)*
(Monitor, and correct as necessary.)

Excellent job writing the letter that makes the /fff/ sound. Now we are going to write two words. Look at the words underneath your line of f's.
Put your finger on the first word. Let's sound it out together.
(Teacher and students:) **/fff/aaa/nnn/**
Read it. fan

Write the word fan on the line. *(Have students say the sounds as they write the letters.)*
(Monitor, and correct as necessary.)

Repeat the process with the word fat.

Good job writing words with the /fff/ sound. I will put a check mark on the Mastery Sheet so we can go to the next activity.

Lesson 15

Activity 7
Letter-Sound Dictation

Let's play another game. I am going to say a sound, and I want you to write the letter that makes the sound as fast as you can. Listen carefully because I am not going to give you much time between sounds.

(Direct students to the bottom section on the activity sheet.) **Get ready.** */d/.* **Write it fast.**
(Pause 4 seconds between each sound. You may want to tap 4 times.)

Next sound. */Nnn/.* *(Pause or tap 4 times.)*

> Repeat the process with the following sounds: /rrr/, /sss/, /mmm/, /aaa/, /t/, /nnn/.

(Scaffold as necessary.)

Good writing. I will put another check mark on the lesson Mastery Sheet. Let's move on to the next activity.

Activity 8
Sounding Out

(When you go through the list of words, distinguish between the letters m and n before sounding out each word.)
(Touch under the n in an.) **What is this letter's sound?** */nnn/*

Sound it out. *(Slide your finger under each letter as students sound out.)* */aaa/nnn/*
Read it fast. an

> Repeat the process with the following words: ant, nat, *sat, **ram.

Note: **(When you come to the word sat, say:)*
The next 2 words have no dots. Sound them out the way you always do.
**(Touch under the m when you come to ram. Follow this procedure:)
What is this letter's sound? */mmm/*
Sound it out. */rrr/aaa/mmm/*
Read it fast. ram

Individual Practice

(Provide individual practice.)

Good reading. What should I do now? Put a check mark on the lesson Mastery Sheet.

an
ant
nat
sat
ram

129 Lesson 15

Activity 9
Connected Text— Teacher Led

Fluency Development

Note: Follow this format: For each tricky word, tap under the word. For each word students can decode, slide your finger under each letter. Students sound out the word and then read it fast. Finally students read each sentence fast. If students hesitate, use the following cues: "Read it" for tricky words, "Sound it out" for decodable words, and "Read it fast" after they sound out the sentence.

We are going to read a story about two rats. When I tap under the tricky words, read them. For the words with the dots, I will slide my finger under the letters, and you will sound them out and then say the words. After you finish sounding out a sentence, read it the fast way.

Note: If students are capable of doing so, they may read the sentences fast the first time. However, students should read and reread the sentences until they can read smoothly and without any mistakes.

Read the first sentence by yourselves today. I /aaa/mmm/ am /Nnn/aaa/t/ Nat. I am Nat.
Great reading. Continue reading.

> **Repeat the process with remaining sentences.**

Look at the last sentence. It has no dots. Read it the same way you always have.
(If students hesitate, use cues.)

Great job reading. Now let's go back to the first sentence and start over. This time, read all the sentences the fast way. Try the first one. I am Nat.

> **Repeat the process with the remaining sentences.**

Individual Practice

(Provide individual practice with 1 sentence per student. Have students repeat the sentence until they can read smoothly.)

Excellent work today, everyone. You have worked together to earn a sticker for your Mastery Sheet.

I am Nat.

I am a ram.

Sam is a rat.

Sam and Nat sat on the mat.

131 Lesson 15

Name _____

Lesson 15

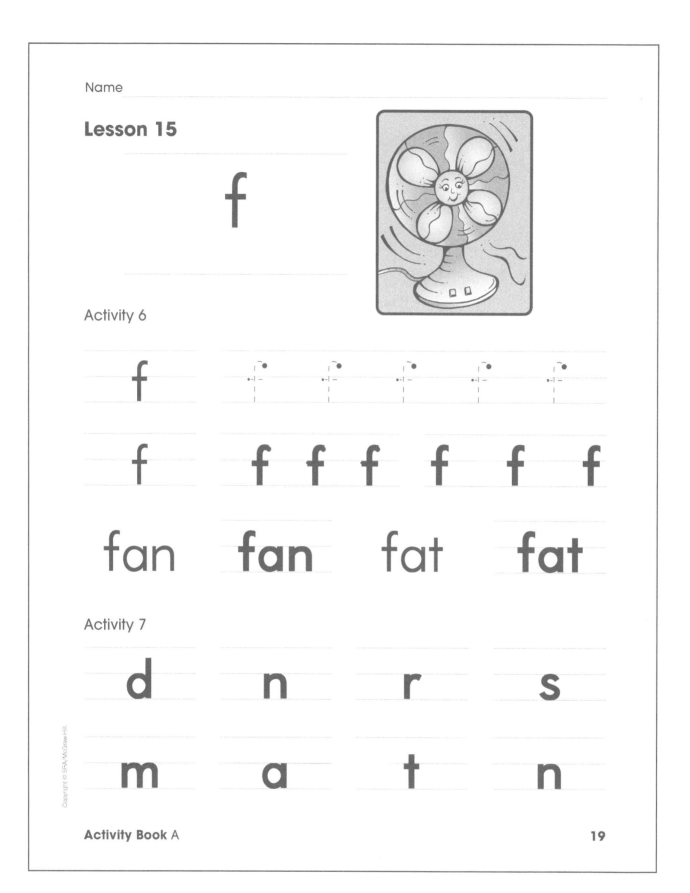

f

Activity 6

f

f   f f f f f f

fan   **fan**   fat   **fat**

Activity 7

d   n   r   s

m   a   t   n

Lesson 71

MATERIALS

1. Letter-Sound Card 33 (or)
2. *Activity Book B,* page 53
3. Marker Board
4. *Story-Time Reader 31, The Stand*
5. Timer

OBJECTIVES

Activity 1 *Word Recognition and Spelling*
- Learn to write and automatically recognize irregular words in stories

Activity 2 *Letter-Sound Correspondences*
- Learn the sound of the letter combination or
- Associate sounds with letters

Activity 3 *Phonemic Awareness*
- Segment spoken words into sounds, and then say words

Activity 4 *Letter-Sound Correspondences*
- Associate sounds with letters

Activity 5 *Word Recognition and Spelling*
- Blend and say word parts to form multisyllabic words

Activity 6 *Word Recognition and Spelling*
- **ELD** Preview words to be read
- Learn to internalize sounding-out procedure to become fluent readers

Activity 7 *Word Recognition and Spelling*
- Blend and say word parts to form multisyllabic words

Activity 8 *Fluency*
- **ELD** Preview words from a story
- Demonstrate the ability to decode text and read words fast
- Build fluency by rereading a story in unison
- Reread a story to meet established fluency goals
- Make and verify predictions, using prior knowledge and picture clues

Activity 1
Tricky Words
Analysis

(Have students turn to page 53 in Activity Book B.)

Note: Teaching students that some letters in tricky words say their sounds correctly will help students when they encounter words they do not know.

Now you will write missing letters in tricky words. Look at the activity sheet. The letters that do *not* say their sounds in each word are written for you. Write the letters that *do* work in each word. Listen as I say each tricky word. Write the letters that say their sounds in the correct order.

I will do the first one. *(Hold up the activity sheet, and point to the first lined space with oul in it.)* **The first word is *would.* The letters *w* and *d,* which are the first and last letters in *would,* say their sounds correctly, so I will write them.** *(Say the word would again as you write the w and the d.)*

Your turn. When I say the word, write the letters that say their sounds correctly. *(Pause.) **Would.** (Pause.)* **Write the letters that work. Say the sounds as you write the letters.**

(Monitor, and scaffold as necessary.)

What word did you write? would

Repeat the process with the following words: does, could, one, four, should, out, for, *of.

Note: *The whole word of does not sound out correctly. Tell students, "This word is of. Neither of the letters in this word says its sound correctly."

**Now let's read all the words together. Say the word when I tap.
First word.** *(Tap.)* would

Repeat the process with the remainder of the words.

Individual Practice
(Provide individual practice.)

We have just finished our first activity. I will mark the Mastery Sheet so we can continue our lesson.

Activity 2
Part A: Letter-Sound Introduction

(Hold up the or letter-sound card.) **These letters usually go together to say /orr/. What sound do these letters usually make together? /orr/**

or

(Direct students to the correct section of the activity sheet.) **Now write the letters that make the /orr/ sound each time I say them. /orr/**

(Monitor, and correct as necessary. Then say /orr/ 5 more times.)

Good. Please keep your activity books open, because we will use them again. Let's continue.

Part B: Thumbs Up—Thumbs Down

Now we will play the Thumbs Up—Thumbs Down game. I will say some words. If you hear the /orr/ sound in a word, give a thumbs-up. If you do not hear the /orr/ sound, put your thumbs down. These words might be tricky because I will say other sounds that are very close to the /orr/ sound.

The first word is *for.*

(Monitor, and correct as necessary.)

Next word. Core.

(Monitor, and correct as necessary.)

Repeat the process with the following words: car, far, fur, form, more, jar, bird, corn, torch, church.

Individual Practice

(Provide individual practice.)

Great job. We have finished this activity. What should I do now?

Activity 3
Stretch and Blend

Now it is time to stretch words and then say them fast.

Fists up. *(Pause.)* **First word. *Order.* Stretch order. /orr/d/err/ What word did you stretch? order**

Repeat the process with the following words: forty, wrong, tenth, barber, salty.

Individual Practice

(Provide individual practice with 1–2 words per student.)

Good work, everyone. You have finished another activity. I will put a check mark on the lesson Mastery Sheet.

Activity 4
Letter-Sound Review

(Hold up the book so all students can see the letters.)

Now it is time to review letter-sounds we have learned so far. When I touch under a letter-sound, tell me its sound. Keep saying its sound until I touch under the next letter-sound.

(Touch under the first y.) **What sound? /yyy/**

Good. Let's continue.

> Repeat the process with the remainder of the letter-sounds.

Individual Practice

(Provide individual practice.)

Great job remembering the letter-sounds. What should I do now?

y a l wh er

ea z p o

y all le ea

w ch sh i

ir wh r e

234 Lesson 71

Lesson 71

Activity 5
Sounding Out

Chunking—Student Led

(Direct students to the correct section of the activity sheet.)

Now you will sound out words on your own. Some words have more than one part. If there is more than one part, sound out each part, and then read the whole word.

(Hold up the activity sheet. Demonstrate by pointing to the word walnut, and say:) **Point to the letter that makes the /www/ sound.** *(Monitor.)*

We are going to read this word in chunks.

(Point to wal.) **Sound out the first part.** *(Tap for each sound in wal.)* **/www/al/**
Say the first part. **wal**

Sound out the second part. *(Tap for each sound in nut.)* **/nnn/uuu/t/**
Say this part. **nut**

Now say the two parts, pointing to each part as you say it. **wal** *(pause)* **nut**
Read the whole word. **walnut**

235 Lesson 71

Repeat the process with the following words: **call, for, fresh, which, churn, forget, glass, butter, *salad, *wants.**

Note: *These two words will be in the story students will read later in this lesson. Remind students that these two words almost sound out right.

Individual Practice

(Provide individual practice.)

You are sounding out and reading words! Excellent!

(Put a check mark on the Mastery Sheet, and continue.)

Activity 6
Reading Fast First

Lists

Language and Literacy Support

During this activity we will be reading some words, and I want to make sure that you understand them all.

The first word is *stiff.* **Who knows what stiff means?** *(If students give another correct meaning for the word, acknowledge it, but focus on the contextual meaning in* **Story-Time Reader 31,** The Stand, *which students will read later in this lesson.)*

(You may have to prompt further by saying:) **Here's a hint. *I must have slept wrong because my neck is stiff this morning.*** *(Accept reasonable responses.)*

That's right. *Stiff* means "hard to move."

The next word is *scarf.* **Does anyone know what a scarf is?** *(You may have to prompt further by saying:)* **What do I mean if I say *I wear a scarf around my neck when it is cold?*** *(Accept reasonable responses.)*

Lesson 71

Yes. A scarf is a piece of cloth or material worn around the shoulders, neck, or head. We usually use scarves to help keep us warm. Here is a picture of a scarf from the story we will be reading. *(Show picture on the cover of The Stand.)* **Have you ever worn a scarf?** *(Accept reasonable responses.)*

Good. The next word is *rent*. Does anyone know what rent means? *(You may have to prompt further by saying:)* **What do I mean if I say *I like to rent videos*?** *(Accept reasonable responses.)*

Yes. To rent means "to pay to use something for a while." If you rent a DVD for the weekend, you pay for the days you are using it, and then you return it.

Good job!

(Pause 1.5 seconds between words to give students time to sound out the words in their heads.)

Here is a list of words you will read fast the first time. I will give you time to sound out the word to yourselves. Then I will say "Read it."

(Touch under the word, and pause 1.5 seconds.) **Read it. stand**

Yes, *stand*. Next word. *(Pause.)* **Read it. fill**

Yes, *fill*. Next word.

> **Repeat the process with the following words: rest, trick, small, stiff, raft, scarf, rent, neck.**

(If students make an error, go back, sound out the word together in a whisper voice, and then say the word fast.)

Individual Practice

(Provide individual practice with 5 words per student. Call on students in random order.)

(Praise, mark the Mastery Sheet, and continue with the next activity.)

Activity 7
Sounding Out

Chunking—Teacher Led

For this activity you will read big words again. When you read these big words, say each part fast the first time. Then read the whole word fast.

(Hold up the word list. Place your finger under the word paddle. Slide your finger under the padd part, and say:) **Say this part. padd**

(Place your finger under the le part, and say:)

Say this part. le

Now say the parts together. *(Touch under each part as students say it.)*

padd *(pause)* **le**
Read the whole word. **paddle**

Repeat the process with the following words: **problem, animals, pocket, carrot, wondered.**

stand

fill

rest

trick

small

stiff

raft

scarf

rent

neck

Staff Development Guide, Level 1

paddle   problem

animals   pocket

carrot   wondered

· ·

Individual Practice

(Give individual turns.)

Now read the words fast the first time. *(Hold up the word list. Place your finger next to the word paddle, and say:)*

First word. *(Pause 3 seconds.)*
Read it. paddle

Repeat the process with the following words: problem, animals, pocket, carrot, wondered.

(Scaffold as necessary, going back to sound out a word if students miss it.)

Individual Practice

(Provide individual practice with 1–2 words per student.)

What a great job reading big words! I will mark the Mastery Sheet, and we can continue. We have only one activity left before our lesson is over.

238 Lesson 71

Activity 8
Story-Time Reader
Fluency Development

FLUENCY GOAL 98 words @ 35 wpm =
2 minutes, 55 seconds

Language and Literacy Support ELD

During this activity we will be reading a story called *The Stand*, and I want to make sure you understand all the words we will be reading.

The first one is actually two words: *step up*. Who knows what step up means?

(You may have to prompt further by saying:) Here's a hint. *The man at the carnival said, "Step up and get your picture taken."* *(Accept reasonable responses.)*

That's right. Step up means come forward. *(Demonstrate by stepping forward.)*

The next one is *step out*. Who knows what step out means? *(You may have to prompt further by saying:)* Here's a hint. *I am sorry I missed you, but I had to step out of my office for a while.* *(Accept reasonable responses.)*

That's right. To step out means "to leave for a short time."

The next word is *trick*. Who knows what trick means? *(If students give another correct meaning, acknowledge it, but focus on the contextual meaning in the selection.)*

(You may have to prompt further by saying:) Here's a hint. *I pushed hard to open the heavy door, and that did the trick.* *(Accept reasonable responses.)*

That's right. Although *trick* often means "to play a mean joke on someone," the word *trick* means something different in our story. When we say something will "do the trick," we mean that it will fix a problem.

Good job!

(Pass out Story-Time Reader 31, The Stand.)

(Write the following words on the marker board: salad, wants.)

Note: Have students read from their books, pointing under each word as they read it. Tap once for each word, allowing enough time between taps for students to sound out decodable words. Use oral cues if necessary.

Before we start reading, let's learn some new words.

The word is *(point to salad) salad.* **What word? salad**

The word is *(point to wants) wants.* **What word? wants**

We are going to read this story fast the first time. If you know the word, say it when I tap. If you do not know a word, sound it out to yourself, and then say it fast when I tap. I will give you time to think before I tap. Remember to follow along by pointing to each word in your book. *(Browse the story. Let students comment on the pictures and make predictions. Have each student make a prediction.)*

Lesson 71

Good. Now we are going to read the story. Get ready. *(Provide think time of 2.5 seconds maximum per word, start the timer, and tap.)* **Step**

Repeat this process for the remainder of the story.

(Review and discuss students' predictions.)

Note: Review any missed words. If students met the fluency goal on the first reading, have them move to Individual Practice. If students did not meet the fluency goal on the first reading, have them read the story a second time in unison. This time have them read the story faster, pausing 2 seconds per word. Then have students complete Individual Practice.

Now you are going to read this story again. This time you will read it faster. *(Pause, start the timer, and tap.)* **Step**

Individual Practice

(Call on individual students to read 1–2 pages. Do not tap during individual practice. Time students as a group. Note on the Mastery Sheet whether the group achieved the fluency goal.)

ERROR CORRECTION:

If students make an error, follow this format: Have students sound out the word together in a whisper voice, read it fast, and then reread the sentence. After students read the story, write each missed word on the board. Have students sound out each word in unison in a whisper voice and then say it fast. Next have students read the list the fast way.

Good job! You have finished today's lesson. I will mark the Mastery Sheet.

240 Lesson 71

Lesson 71

Activity 1

oul	oes	oul
o e	our	oul
ou	or	of

Activity 2

Activity 5

walnut   call   for

fresh   which   churn

forget   glass   butter

salad   wants

Lesson 101

MATERIALS

1. Letter-Sound Card 35 (A—vowel)
2. *Activity Book C*, page 40
3. *Story-Time Reader 49, Steve's Secret*
4. Stopwatch and Timer
5. Marker Board
   ELD *Pictures for Language and Literacy Support,* page 112

OBJECTIVES

Activity 1 *Letter-Sound Correspondences*
• Learn the long a sound spelled *ai* and *ay*
• Associate sounds with letters

Activity 2 *Letter-Sound Correspondences*
• Associate sounds with letters

Activity 3 *Phonemic Awareness*
• Develop automatic discrimination between long- and short-vowel sounds

Activity 4 *Word Recognition and Spelling*
• Blend and say word parts to form multisyllabic words

Activity 5 *Fluency*
ELD Preview words from a story
• Demonstrate the ability to decode text and read words fast
• Reread a story to meet established fluency goals
• Build fluency by rereading a story in unison
• Make and verify predictions, using prior knowledge and picture clues
• Build fluency by rereading a story with a partner

Activity 6 *Comprehension Strategies*
• Identify the main idea of a story in 10 words or fewer

Note: Starting at this point in the program, students no longer sound out words aloud.

(Write on the marker board any letter-sounds or words students had trouble with on Assessment 15. Using the model-lead-test strategy, review the letter-sounds and words with students.)

Activity 1
Letter-Sound Introduction

*(Hold up the **A—vowel** letter-sound card, and touch under* a_e.) **What sound?** /aaa/

Very good. Now you will learn two new ways to spell this letter's name.

(Touch under ai.) **Sometimes /aaa/ is written with these letters.**

Your turn. What sound do you say when you see these letters? /aaa/

(Touch under ay.) **Sometimes /aaa/ is written with these letters.**

What sound do you say when you see these letters? /aaa/

Individual Practice

(Give individual turns with both spellings.)

Good. Now you will read some words together that have /aaa/ written the new way.

(Touch under ai on the next page.) **What sound? /aaa/**

First word. Read the underlined part. /aaa/ What word? bait

Yes, *bait.* Let's continue.

Repeat the process with the following words: maid, train, main, stain, paint.

Very good. *(Touch under ay on the next page.)* **What sound do these letters make? /aaa/**

First word. Read the underlined part. /aaa/ What word? day

Yes, *day.* Let's continue.

Repeat the process with the following words: say, bay, away, may, today.

Individual Practice

(Provide individual practice with at least 1 word from each column.)

(Praise students, mark off the activity on the Mastery Sheet, and continue.)

139 Lesson 101

ai

bait

maid

train

main

stain

paint

ay

day

say

bay

away

may

today

Activity 2
Letter-Sound Review

It's time to review letter-sounds you have learned so far.

Repeat the process with the remaining letter-sounds.

(Remember to have students read from left to right across the page.)

(Touch under e_e.) **What sound?** /ēēē/

Good. Let's continue.

Note: If a letter-sound represents more than 1 sound, ask, "What sound do you try first? What sound do you try next?"

For *ge, gi, ce,* and *ci,* ask, "What sound does this letter make *(Touch under g or c.)* when it is followed by this letter?" *(Touch under e or i.)*

(Follow the usual correction procedure.)

Individual Practice

(Provide individual practice.)

Good job reading the letter-sounds. I will mark the Mastery Sheet, and we can continue with the next activity.

e e_e ol u_e v ci

gi a_e ir y l

r sh x ing er

ce ge th ea ee

Activity 3
Vowel Sounds

CVC and VCe

Everyone, tell me the rule about the silent e. If there is an e at the end of a word, the vowel says its name.

Now let's read some words. Check for an e on the end of these words.

(Touch under Steve.) First word. *(Pause.)* Say the underlined part. /eee/ Read the word. **Steve**

> **Repeat the process with the following words: smile, stone, with, hid, will, white, shade, shave, flat, red, size, Eve, but.**

Now let's read these words fast the first time. When I touch under a word, read it.

(Touch under Steve.) Read it. **Steve**

> **Repeat the process with the following words: smile, stone, with, hid, will, white, shade, shave, flat, red, size, Eve, but.**

Individual Practice

(Give individual turns.)

(Praise students, mark off the activity on the Mastery Sheet, and continue.)

141 Lesson 101

Steve

stone

hid

white

shave

red

Eve

smile

with

will

shade

flat

size

but

Activity 4
Sounding Out
Chunking—Student Led

(Have students turn to page 40 in Activity Book C. Remind students that when a word or a syllable ends in a vowel, the vowel usually says its name.)

Everyone, touch the first word.

(Pause 2 seconds.) **Read the first part. se**

(Pause 2 seconds.) **Read the next part. cret**

(Pause 2 seconds.) **Read the whole word. secret**

Repeat the process with the following words: pocket, acorn, dragon, dragons, terrible, *tickled, little, even, fever.

Note: *If students have trouble with tickled, cover the d, and have them read tickle first.

Now you will read these words fast.

Everyone, touch the first word. *(Pause 2 seconds.)*

Read it. **secret**

Yes, *secret.* Next word.

Repeat the process with the following words: pocket, acorn, dragon, dragons, terrible, tickled, little, even, fever.

(Scaffold as necessary.)

Individual Practice

(Give individual turns with 2–3 words per student.)

(Praise students, mark off the activity on the Mastery Sheet, and continue.)

Activity 5
Story-Time Reader

Part A: Unison Reading

Language and Literacy Support

During this activity we will be reading a story, and I want to make sure you understand all the words we will be reading.

The first word is **acorn.** Who knows what an acorn is? *(If students give another correct meaning, acknowledge it, but focus on the contextual meaning in the story.)*

(You may have to prompt further by saying:) **Here's a hint. The squirrel gathered acorns that had fallen from the tree.** *(Accept reasonable responses.)*

That's right. An acorn is a nut from an oak tree. Here is a picture of an acorn. *(Hold up Pictures for Language and Literacy Support, page 112.)*

Next is the sentence *Let me be.* Who knows what *let me be* means? *(You may have to prompt further by saying:)* **Here's a hint. Please don't talk to me; just let me be.** *(Accept reasonable responses.)*

Good. *Let me be* is another way to say "leave me alone."

Who remembers what *shade* means? *(Accept reasonable responses.)* That's right. Shade is darkness from the sun caused by a shadow.

In today's story, *shade* has a different meaning. What do I mean if I say *Your shirt is a beautiful shade of blue?* *(Accept reasonable responses.)*

Yes. *Shade* in this case means a color that is a little different from others in the same color group. Light blue, dark blue, and bright blue are all shades of blue.

Nice job!

(Pass out **Story-Time Reader 49,** Steve's Secret, *to students.)*

FLUENCY GOAL 111 words @ 50 wpm = 2 minutes, 20 seconds

Everyone, point to the title of our story. Each time I tap, read a word.

(Tap for each word in the title.) **Steve's Secret**

What do you think this story is about? *(Allow students to make predictions for no longer than 1 minute. Set a purpose for reading, such as checking to see if these predictions are correct.)*

Now we are going to read the story together the fast way. *(Start timer.)* **First word.** *(Provide think time of 1–1.5 seconds maximum per word, start the timer, and tap.)* **Steve**

> **Repeat this process for the remainder of the story. Error correction procedures: If an error occurs, have students sound out the word in a whisper voice, read the word, and then reread the sentence. Do not stop the timer during corrections.**

(Review any missed words. Write the words on the board. Have students sound out each word in a whisper voice and then say it fast. Then have students read the list the fast way.)

(Review students' predictions.)

Note: If the group meets the fluency goal on the first read, have students complete Part B. If the group does not meet the fluency goal on the first read, have students read the story again in unison, even faster. Then have students complete Part B.

(Review any missed words. Write the words on the board. Have students sound out each word in a whisper voice and then say it fast. Then have students read the list the fast way. Proceed to Part B.)

Part B: Partner Reading:
Beat the Clock

Now we are going to play Beat the Clock. You will take turns reading the story one page at a time as fast as you can without making mistakes, until you have read the whole story. You will try to read the story all the way through before time runs out.

(Assign partners and the first reader in each pair. Pair yourself with a different reader for this lesson.)

Everyone, turn to the first page of our story, and get ready to read. You have 2 minutes and 20 seconds to read the story. First readers, begin reading. *(Time students for 2 minutes, 20 seconds.)*

(When time runs out, say:) **Stop. Good job. Did you beat the clock?**

(Monitor to see what page each pair was able to finish. Praise all students for doing a good job reading.)

Good job reading the story! I will mark the Mastery Sheet, and we can continue with the last activity in the lesson.

(Mark off this activity on the Mastery Sheet, and continue. On the Mastery Sheet, record the name of your partner and whether he or she met the fluency goal for this activity, and note whether students met the fluency goal as a group.)

Activity 6
Main Idea

Let's talk about Steve's Secret. What is this story mainly about? *(Discuss briefly.)*

Do you think we can say the main idea in fewer words? I think we can. *(Pause to see if students can restate the main idea in fewer words.)*

Now listen as I try. Count how many words I use. *(Monitor.)*
Steve has a secret he doesn't want to share.

Note: Follow this process for determining the main idea:

1. Ask whom or what the story is mainly about.

2. Ask what is important about the main person, place, or thing in the story.

Good job remembering our story. We have finished the lesson, and you know what that means!

TEACHER'S GUIDE

1. Whom is our story about? Steve
2. What is important about Steve in our story? He has a secret.
3. Main idea: Steve has a secret he doesn't want to share.

Lesson 101

Activity 4

<u>secr</u>et	<u>po</u>cket
<u>a</u>corn	<u>dra</u>gon
<u>dra</u>gons	<u>terri</u>ble
<u>tick</u>led	<u>littl</u>e
<u>e</u>ven	<u>fe</u>ver

Activity Book C

Troubleshooting

Problem: Students do not respond on cue.

Solution: Remind students to answer together on cue. If the problem persists, discuss the importance of responding on cue. Remind students that answering together gives them all the opportunity to answer each question.

Use the basic correction technique Model-Lead-Test. Model the correct way to answer on cue. Have the students practice it with you. Then have the students do it on their own. The best way to make sure students continue to answer on cue is to make sure they do it every time.

Problem: One student answers before the cue.

Solution: Validate the student for knowing the answer. Enlist the student to be your helper. Explain how helping means answering on cue. Review the importance of the group answering together.

If a student seems to want individual attention, remind the student that everyone has the opportunity to answer by themselves during individual practice. If this does not resolve the problem, then access Model-Lead-Test. Model answering on cue, have students practice with you, and then have them do it on their own. Your expectation needs to be consistent.

Problem: A student answers slightly behind the cue.

Solution: Praise the students who responded on cue. When a student answers slightly behind the cue, it usually means he or she does not really know the answer. Treat this as a normal error, and correct with the Model-Test strategy. If a student is consistently behind the cue, increase the think time between cues.

Problem: A student does not hold a continuous sound or mispronounces a sound.

Solution: Mispronouncing sounds causes problems for students when they are decoding and spelling words. Correct using the Model-Lead-Test strategy. Model the correct way to say the sound. Have students say the sound with you. Have students say the sound in unison without you, back up two or three items, and begin the task again.

Problem: A student reads a word fast rather than sounding it out first.

Solution: Validate the student: "I'm glad you can read that word fast." Restate the task: "Now show me that you can sound it out, one sound at a time." If the student is still unable to sound out the word, do a Model-Lead-Test.

Problem: Students misspell a word.

Solution: A student misspells a word, for example, *fats* instead of *fast.* Have student stretch the word. **Stretch *fast.*** Students stretch the word, holding up one finger for each sound in the word. **Does the order of your letters match the order of the sounds?** If this is not sufficient, have the student point to each letter as you stretch *fast,* and have the student identify what sound does not match. Continue prompting until the student spells the whole word correctly.

Problem: Students consistently experience difficulty in achieving mastery.

Solution: Back up a few lessons. Students are not firm on previously presented content. It can be normal for struggling students to master a skill one day and then be unable to demonstrate mastery over the same skill the next day, which is why skills are practiced each day. That is also why it is important for students to achieve true lesson mastery before moving to the next lesson.

Problem: One student in a group is having difficulty keeping up with the other students.

Solution: Regroup if possible. Provide a few minutes of one-on-one instruction. Integrate easier items into activities to ensure that the struggling student feels successful.

Problem: A student refuses to work.

Solution: A student may be reluctant to work at first because he or she is unsure of what is expected, because he or she may not know the answer, or because he or she may be afraid to make a mistake. Create a positive, nurturing environment. Add external motivators such as stickers. Play the Beat the Teacher Game. The students get a point every time they follow directions. However, if anyone in the group does not follow directions, you get a point.

Problem: You find yourself telling one student to sit up and another student to listen.

Solution: Reestablish rules. Examine your pacing. You may be too slow or inconsistent.

Students engage in off-task behavior when they aren't sure what is expected of them, if the pace is inappropriate, or if the material is too difficult. Reestablish the rules so students know what is expected of them. A quick reminder, such as Sit tall, Listen big, Answer on my cue, may be necessary every now and then.

Good pacing keeps students engaged in the lesson. Poor pacing results in off-task behavior. Prepare materials ahead of time, and have them within reach. The transition from one activity to the next should be smooth with no downtime, so you don't have to reorganize students between activities.

Do not underestimate the impact of mastery on behavior management. Students who experience continual success are more confident and stay engaged. If students don't meet mastery criterion, it will become harder and harder for them to experience success. This can lead to frustration that masquerades as poor behavior.

Problem: Your students are not meeting their fluency goals on *Story-Time Readers.*

Solution: Use choral reading and echo reading to help students meet goals.

If students consistently struggle to meet fluency goals, reflect on your teaching. Do you stop students when they miss a word while they are reading and have them sound it out and read it fast? Do you have them then go back and reread the sentence? After they finish reading the story, do you review missed words? Do you require each student to achieve individual mastery on the list of missed words before they reread the story?

If you are doing all these things, then you may need to use an additional technique. In choral reading, you read aloud with the students. Read the text at the desired fluency rate. Students attempt to keep up with you. Then students read again without you but at the same rate.

Echo reading is best used when you want to model how the text should sound. First you read a page, and then students read the page at the same rate. Once students have mastered each page, they should be able to meet the fluency goal for the entire story.

Glossary

Alphabetic Pertaining to a writing system that uses a symbol for each speech sound of the language. Of, relating to, or expressed by an alphabet.

Alphabetic Principle Use of letters and letter combinations to represent phonemes in an orthography. Refers to the fact that each sound in the English language has a graphic representation.

Blending Auditory skill that increases phonological awareness of the sound structure of words. After a word is stretched by the teacher, the students are asked to put the sounds together and say the word at a normal rate. For example, the teacher says /mmm/aaa/t/, and the students say *mat.* Blending allows the students an extended period of time to hear the smaller units of sound contained in a word. Blending is also referred to as "telescoping a word."

Co-articulated Spoken together so that separate segments are not easily detected.

Comprehension Mental act of knowing when one does and does not understand what one is reading.

Consonant Phoneme that is not a vowel and is formed with obstruction of the flow of air with the teeth, lips, or tongue.

Consonant Digraph Written letter combination that corresponds to one speech sound but is not represented by either letter alone. Examples: *th, ph, sh, tch.*

Continuous Sound Letter-sound that can be held without distorting the sound. Examples: *a, e, f, i, l, m, n, o, r, s, u, v, w, y, z.*

Decodable Text Text in which a large proportion of the words (70 to 80 percent) are made up of letter-sound relationships that have already been taught.

Decoding Ability to translate a word from print to speech. The act of deciphering a new word by sounding it out.

Decoding Units Distinct parts that text can be broken into, including letter-sounds, words, phrases, and sentences.

Digraph Two or three consecutive letters that represent one sound. There are both vowel digraphs and consonant digraphs. Examples: *th, sh, wh, tch, ai, ay, ir, igh, ea, ee, aw.*

Diphthong Complex speech sound that begins with one vowel sound and gradually changes to another vowel sound within the same syllable. Examples: /oi/ in *oil* and /ou/ in *house.*

Flex Word Word that almost sounds out in a familiar way. Most of the letters in a flex word represent their most common sounds. The word sounds out close enough that the students can figure out the correct pronunciation.

Grapheme Letter or letter combination that spells a single phoneme. In English a grapheme may be 1, 2, 3, or 4 letters, such as *e, ei, igh, eigh.*

Multisyllabic Having more than one syllable.

Orthography Phoneme Writing system. Speech sound that combines with others in a language system to make words; the smallest phonetic unit in a language that is capable of conveying a distinction in meaning.

Phoneme Awareness (or Phonemic Awareness) The conscious awareness that words are made up of segments of our own speech and are represented with letters in an alphabetic orthography.

Phonics Study of the relationships between letters and the sounds they represent; sound-symbol correspondences. Refers to the system by which symbols represent sounds in an alphabetic writing system.

Phonological Awareness Conscious awareness and knowledge that words are composed of separate sounds or phonemes. Ability to manipulate these phonemes in words.

Phonology Rule system within a language by which phonemes are sequenced and uttered to make words; study of the unconscious rules that govern speech-sound production.

***r*-controlled** Pertaining to a vowel immediately followed by the consonant *r,* such that its pronunciation is affected, or even dominated, by the /*r*/ sound.

Reading Fluency Speed of reading, including effortless, accurate, and smooth reading with expression.

Schwa Nondistinct vowel found in unstressed syllables in English.

Scope and Sequence The "scope" refers to the amount or range of information contained in the curriculum. "Sequence" is the order in which the information and/or skills are presented.

Segmenting Auditory skill that helps students hear the discrete sounds within a word. The teacher says the word at a normal rate, and students are asked to segment it into its individual phonemes. Each continuous sound in a word is held for two seconds, switching from sound to sound without pausing. Stop sounds within the word are said quickly so as not to distort their sound. Segmenting is also referred to as "stretching a word."

Sounding Out Matching a letter-sound to its graphic representation. Starting at the beginning of the word, the students say the sound corresponding to the first letter. Students advance in a left-to-right progression, saying the sound for each successive letter. The sounds are said one after another without stopping between the sounds.

Stop Sounds Consonant speech sound that is articulated with a stop of the airstream. The sound cannot be held without distortion. Example: *b, c, d, g, h, j, k, p, q, t.*

Stretch and Blend Phonological awareness activity that requires students to combine the blending and segmenting exercises. The teacher says a word at the normal rate, the students stretch the word into its individual phonemes, and then students say the word at the normal rate.

Syllable Unit of pronunciation that is organized around a vowel. It may or may not have consonants before or after the vowel.

Tricky Words (Sight Words) Words taught as whole words and explained as not following the regular sound-spelling rules.

Unstressed Unaccented syllable within a word.

Voiced Speech sound articulated with vibrating vocal cords.

Vowel Open phoneme that is the nucleus of every syllable and is classified by tongue position and height, such as high/low or front/mid/back. English has eighteen vowel phonemes.